HOW TO CALCULATE DIVERSITY RETURN-ON-INVESTMENT

A Step-by-Step Toolkit for Linking Diversity Initiatives to the Bottom-line

By Edward E. Hubbard, Ph.D.

How To Calculate Diversity Return On Investment (DROI)

Library of Congress Catalog Card Number: 99-97627

ISBN 1-883733-21-9

Cover design by Dolores Gillum, Kathexis Design

Global Insights Publishing
1302 Holm Road
Petaluma, CA 94954
Office: (707) 763-8380   Fax: (707) 763-3640

Preface

Preface

Introduction

There is a common saying that indicates "you can't manage what you don't measure" and this is certainly true when it comes to diversity. Measuring the results of diversity initiatives will become a key strategic requirement to demonstrate its contribution to organizational performance. Diversity professionals and managers know they must begin to show how diversity is linked to the bottom-line in hard numbers or they will have difficulty maintaining funding, gaining support, and assessing progress. Although interest in measuring the effects of diversity has been growing, the topic still challenges even the most sophisticated and progressive diversity departments.

In my previous book, *Measuring Diversity Results (Global Insights Publishing—1997)*, I discussed some of the foundational skills, techniques, and formulas you can use to measure the success of your diversity initiatives. In this book, I will help you learn an entire process to analyze, measure, track, and report a specific diversity initiative to demonstrate its value. The measurement approaches used in this book are both practical and comprehensive. Most of the steps in the process involve using common, well-known processes and basic arithmetic. Its primary focus as a *"learning toolkit"* is to help you calculate Diversity's Return-on-Investment (DROI) using effective measurement strategies to assess diversity's impact on business results.

The DROI method utilizes a seven-step process for measuring, analyzing, interpreting and reporting your progress. The process links strategic organizational objectives and work process flow to diversity performance and key impact metrics. This book gives you step-by-step instructions, worksheets and examples to help you analyze the impact of your diversity initiatives in the context of the work you do on a day-to-day basis.

The first half of the book walks you through the process one step at a time. Each step is explained and demonstrated with examples. Then, you are given opportunities to practice the step. The second half of the book is designed as a reference you can use to understand key concepts in further detail, learn about new computerized diversity measurement tools and techniques to build a financial performance mindset.

In this book, I will show you how to:

- Link diversity measures to key organizational performance measures

- Implement a multi-step process to evaluate diversity's impact and contribution
- Identify key analysis questions to use to frame and guide a comprehensive diversity measurement study of an important business issue
- Collect diversity-related data that highlights the contribution of diversity to the organization's bottom-line
- Use a specific data isolation technique to identify the contribution of diversity from other elements
- Convert diversity's contribution to dollars
- Calculate diversity's costs and benefits
- Report the diversity metrics demonstrating its contribution and return-on-investment.
- Plan ways to track each diversity measure

I will also identify diversity software measurement tools, standard and customizable survey methods you can use, and explain key concepts and techniques such as:

- The Causal Model of Diversity Management Climate, Performance and Results
- The Diversity Contribution Model and Calculation
- And much more....

In essence, this book is designed for anyone who would like a concrete roadmap with detailed instructions to design, measure, analyze, and/or improve his or her diversity initiatives and demonstrate its financial return on investment.

I hope you will find this book to be an invaluable resource in your efforts to demonstrate the key strategic value of diversity as a competitive edge in business performance.

Acknowledgements

My first and deepest appreciation goes to my beautiful, caring wife, Myra. Your love, support, and helpful perspectives along the way made this work possible. You give me the hope and courage to continue to do this work in spite of the difficulties and challenges. This book is dedicated to you.

Secondly, I would like to thank my wonderful family. My mother, Geneva Hubbard whose love and encouragement always keeps me strong and whose wisdom is so vast its immeasurable. To my sisters and their families as well as a host of relatives who always kept me in their prayers. And to many others…Thank You.

There are a number of people, whether they know it or not, who made the completion of this book possible. Some of them provided their scholarly works. Others provided personal encouragement.

I am again indebted to the many scholars on measurement such as Jack J. Phillips, Jac Fitz-enz, Donald Kirkpatrick, Wayne Casio, Jack Zigon, Lyle Spencer, Carl Thor, Ron Zemke, and others too numerous to mention. Their thought-provoking research help shape some of the major processes utilized in this return on investment approach. Thank you for sharing your knowledge such that others can learn and grow.

I am particularly indebted to several diversity professionals. Kay Iwata, Julie O'Mara, R. Roosevelt Thomas, Juan Lopez, Jeff Howard, David Tulin, Lynda White, Jay Lucas, Marilyn French-Hubbard, Pat Harbour, Steven Davis, Price Cobbs, Steve Hanamura, Robert Hayles, Peggy Riley, Emilio Egea, Ignace Conic, Ed McDonnell, Milfred (Fred) Moore, Barbara Clark-Evans, Hershel Herndon, Mary C. Gentile, Dwight Herrera, Marshall Maez, and Kim Cromwell. I would also like to thank all of the members of the Diversity Collegium, participant in the many Hubbard Diversity Measurement & Productivity Institute programs, particularly the "Measuring Diversity Results" and Building a Measurable Diversity Strategic Plan workshops, and others too numerous to name.

To my friend, Dolores Gillum of Kathexis Designs for her brilliant, creative work on everything she touches. You are truly gifted as is evident in the designs of the book dust jacket and other literature you have created from our conversations or my scribbling. Thank you for your hard work.

And of course, to our tremendous Hubbard & Hubbard, Inc., staff, particularly Sheryl Casteen, Karen D'Angelo, and Edward E. Hubbard II whose support and hard work helped keep things running smoothly during this period.

In any work like this, there are many people whose contributions deserve recognition that I may have overlooked. Please forgive me if I missed you in this list. Thank you all for your guidance and support.

Edward E. Hubbard
Petaluma, California

Contents

Contents

How to Calculate Diversity ROI

Contents

How to Use This Toolkit

How to Use This Toolkit

What this Toolkit Is About

If the language of business is dollars, then the alphabet is numbers. All organizations, whether profit or non-profit, depend on their ability to get the best possible return on dollars invested.

This toolkit is designed to help you learn a successful process to measure and track the organization's diversity investment. The diversity measurement approach used in this toolkit will be both practical and comprehensive. Most of the steps in the process will involve using common, well-known processes and basic arithmetic. Its primary focus is to help you calculate Diversity Return-on-Investment (DROI).

This toolkit describes a seven-step process for measuring, analyzing, interpreting and reporting your diversity results and its impact on the organization's bottom-line.

Who Should Use This Toolkit

This toolkit is written for anyone who wants to analyze, measure, demonstrate, and/or improve their diversity initiatives' impact, such as…

➢ Diversity Council members
➢ Workforce Diversity Directors and Managers

How to Calculate Diversity ROI

➢ Global Diversity Executives

➢ Vice Presidents of Human Resources

➢ EEO and Affirmative Action Executives

➢ CEOs

➢ COOs

➢ Organization Development Specialists

➢ Etc.

This toolkit is designed to help you learn how to implement a formal measurement process to demonstrate diversity's return-on-investment impact in the least possible time. It will act as your coach and guide while providing a place for you to record your implementation ideas as you execute this process.

Purpose of This Toolkit

After working through this toolkit, you will be able to:

What You Will Learn

➢ Link diversity measures to the organization's measures of performance

➢ Implement a multi-step process to evaluate diversity's impact and contribution

➢ Identify key analysis questions to use to frame and guide a comprehensive diversity measurement study of an important business issue

➢ Collect diversity-related data that highlights the contribution of diversity to the organizational bottom-line

> ➢ Use a specific data isolation technique to identify the contribution of diversity to organizational objectives
>
> ➢ Convert diversity's contribution to dollars
>
> ➢ Calculate diversity's costs and benefits
>
> ➢ Report the diversity metrics demonstrating its contribution and return-on-investment
>
> ➢ Plan how to track each diversity measure

What this Toolkit Contains

This *"How to Calculate Diversity Return-on-Investment Toolkit"* contains step-by-step instructions, worksheets and examples to help you analyze the impact of your diversity initiatives in the context of organizational goals and objectives.

The first half of the toolkit walks you through the process one step at a time. Each step is explained and demonstrated with examples. Then you are given opportunities to practice the step. The second half is a reference you can use to build your knowledge and skills.

Your Situation	What to Do
You are helping others in the organization analyze diversity's contribution in their area	<ul><li>**Distribute** copies of this book to your diversity team members and key contact members in the departments you are working with.</li><li>**Learn** the techniques before trying to assist others. Use the exercises and a well-known diversity initiative area such as diversity training, diversity hiring or recruitment as practice material for learning the skills.</li><li>**Guide** the members of your diversity measurement team through the steps in the process slowly and with reflection on advantages for other parts of the organization.</li></ul>
You and your diversity team are working together to create metrics for diversity initiatives under your immediate control	<ul><li>**Distribute** copies of this book to your diversity team members.</li><li>**Work** through the exercises together as a group. Skip the generic exercises and move straight to the "Application Exercises" if you are pressed for time.</li></ul>

Your Situation	What to Do
	• **Use** sub-teams to create drafts that can be discussed among diversity team members to avoid getting bogged down in unproductive sessions.
You are completing this toolkit alone	• **Complete** the exercises alone but seek out someone with whom to discuss the answers. This "reality check" is helpful when you get lost in the details of measuring your diversity initiatives and their impact. • **Optional:** Contact Hubbard & Hubbard, Inc. for consultation support to help you work through the process.
You are in the *How to Calculate DROI Workshop*: How to Calculate Diversity Return-on-Investment	• **Complete** the exercises as directed by your Hubbard & Hubbard, Inc. facilitator.

How to Calculate Diversity ROI

This icon is a signal for you to do something. In general you will be asked to complete one of two kinds of exercises.

What to Do Next

Those marked "Practice Exercises" will give you an opportunity to *practice* what you have read about in the preceding pages. Your practice will be directed towards a case study situation.

Those marked "Application Exercises" will give you an opportunity to *apply* what you've learned to your organization's diversity pilot study or formal measurement study. You will use your real life organization goals and objectives as the basis for your efforts.

In either case you will be given some assistance in determining if the work you've done is correct.

Overview

Overview

Challenges In Diversity Measurement

Diversity performance is challenging to measure for the following reasons:

➤ It is not always obvious what results should be measured. Many diversity organizations will not use any measures at all or they will use the obvious measures without asking what results they should be producing and how they will know when they have done a good job.

➤ Even if you know what to measure, it is often not clear how the measurement process should be conducted. Not everything can be easily measured with numbers, thus the diversity practitioner may give up when faced with measuring something like "creativity" or "diverse work team productivity" or "innovation".

➤ Diversity impacts individuals, teams, the organization, customer markets, and communities at large. Therefore measurements must be done at all of these levels, which has an exponential effect on the size of the measurement task. Portions of this measurement task can be complex and difficult without direction.

How to Calculate Diversity ROI

This approach will:

➤ Provide a road map for this difficult measurement task. It is easy to get lost when the task is as hard as measuring the impact of diversity on organizational performance. If you have a process, you can focus on getting to the goal instead of deciding on what steps are the best to take next.

➤ Help you reduce the cycle time to create diversity measures and perform a diversity measurement study. Organizations have spent months and virtually years trying to create measures and processes to evaluate the contribution of diversity to the bottom-line. This process will help you cut that time down into weeks or days.

➤ Provide a way to measure the "difficult to measure" work. It will also suggest ways to acquire and create performance standards for diversity.

➤ Help you link diversity goals to the goals and objectives of the organization. Line of sight helps motivation, but it can be difficult to achieve. Employees and stakeholders must be able to see how diversity activities and results will help the organization achieve its goals and objectives. The process must also help employees know what's required of them to reach the organization's goals.

➢ Provide a way to combine diversity and organizational measures such that they support each other and do not work at cross-purposes.

➢ Provide options for varying the process, given the type of organizational work or process being measured.

End Point of the Process

Because there are many different aspects of diversity applications in organizations, the diversity measurement process is not always linear. You'll need to have a clear understanding of the organization's business operations, its strategic focus and challenges, and where you want to end up. As you proceed with the diversity measurement study, you must make choices along the way to find the most efficient path to help reach your goal.

For most diversity organizations, the goal is to demonstrate diversity's contribution to the organization's bottom-line and utilize a measurement system that everyone involved can understand. It must delineate what is expected of them in the process and provide tools and helpful hints along the way to achieve a successful outcome. To that end, this process will help you:

➢ Build a business case for a specific diversity initiative's contribution.
➢ Create a roadmap of consideration made along the way.

How to Calculate Diversity ROI

➢ Utilize tools that support consistency in analysis and performance tracking.

➢ Show value-added results with diversity measures and performance standards.

The example shown below highlights a portion of a diversity value chain that reflects value-added results, standards, diversity metrics and their impact that may be suggested.

Example of Diversity Value-Chain Analysis

Value-Added Results/ Weight%	Diversity Performance Standards	Diversity Metric(s) / Target	Organization Impact
Business Unit Diversity Teams (25%)	▪ Diversity Best Practices mirrored at the business unit level	▪ Diversity Best Practices mirrored at the business unit level ▪ At least a 25% increase in customer satisfaction due to diversity intervention	▪ Improved Customer Service
Staffing (20%)	▪ Diversity source cost reduced ▪ Diversity hire retention by group is increased ▪ Diversity hire performance impact and quality is tracked	▪ Less than 20day Time-to-fill Rate ▪ % Reduction in Source cost per diversity hire ▪ At least a 95% Diversity hit rate ▪ At least a 90% Diversity hire performance impact ▪ 90% Diversity survival rate ▪ 92% Diversity stability factor ▪ Target increase (#/%) of minority and women promoted by category and level ▪ Cost/Benefit of Turnover Reduction	▪ Diverse workforce reflective of customer and local population demographics

**Overview
of the
Steps to
Calculate
Diversity
ROI**

There are seven steps to calculate Diversity Return-on-Investment:

1. **Know what you want to know**. This step will help you:
   - Identify a Business Problem Related to the Organization's Strategy
   - Formulate Research Questions
   - Begin with the End in Mind -- Your Report
   - Create the Diversity Measurement Study Objectives

2. **Prepare and Collect data.** This step will help you:
   - Identify Data Collection Measurement Areas to Check
   - Review Historical Data
   - Conduct Interviews
   - Conduct Focus Groups
   - Analyze data using the Hubbard Diversity 9-S Framework
   - Create or Purchase Evaluation Instruments
   - Survey the Organization

3. **Isolate diversity's contribution**. This step will help you:
   - Select a Method to Isolate Diversity's Contribution

4. **Convert the contribution to money**. This step will help:
   - Identify the Hard and Soft Data Contained in the Diversity Contribution

➤ Select a Method to Convert the Hard Data Contribution to Dollars

5. **Calculate the costs, benefits and DROI.** This step will help you:
  - ➤ Identify the Major Cost Categories
  - ➤ Identify the Major Benefits
  - ➤ Calculate the Benefit-to-Cost Ratio
  - ➤ Calculate the Diversity Return-on-Investment (DROI %)
  - ➤ Identify the Intangible Benefits

6. **Report it to others.** This step will help you:
  - ➤ Identify the Report Timing / Other Needs
  - ➤ Identify Reporting Vehicle(s)
  - ➤ Create Report
  - ➤ Deliver Report
  - ➤ Evaluate Feedback

7. **Track and periodically assess progress.** This step will:
  - ➤ Provide follow-up data for analysis and benchmarking purposes
  - ➤ Introduce new automated Diversity Measurement Software Systems for monitoring, tracking, and reporting results
  - ➤ Introduce a companion survey development software tool and its statistical analysis capabilities

Introduction to the Diversity Return On Investment Process

Introduction to the Diversity ROI Process

Introduction

Measuring the results of diversity initiatives will become a key strategic requirement to demonstrate its contribution to organizational goals and objectives. Diversity professionals and managers know they must begin to show how diversity is linked to the bottom-line in hard numbers. In short, they must calculate and report their **diversity return-on-investment**. To get off to a good start, let's begin our journey by defining what we mean when we use the term "diversity".

What do we mean when we say "diversity"?

When I use the term *"Diversity"*, I define it as a collective mixture characterized by differences and similarities that are applied in pursuit of organizational objectives. I define *"Diversity Management"* as the process of planning for, organizing, directing, and supporting these collective mixtures in a way that adds a measurable difference to organizational performance.

Diversity and its mixtures can be organized into four interdependent and sometimes overlapping aspects: Workforce

How to Calculate Diversity ROI

Diversity, Behavioral Diversity, Structural Diversity, and Business Diversity.

Workforce Diversity encompasses group and situational identities of the organization's employees (i.e., gender, race, ethnicity, religion, sexual orientation, physical ability, age, family status, economic background and status, and geographical background and status). It also includes changes in the labor market demographics.

Behavioral Diversity encompasses work styles, thinking styles, learning styles, communication styles, aspirations, beliefs/value system as well as changes in the attitudes and expectation on the part of employees.

Structural Diversity encompasses interactions across functions, across organizational levels in the hierarchy, across divisions and between parent companies and subsidiaries, across organizations engaged in strategic alliances and cooperative ventures. As organizations attempt to become more flexible, less layered, more team-based, and more multi- and cross-functional, measuring this type of diversity will require more attention.

Business Diversity encompasses the expansion and segmentation of customer markets, the diversification of products and services offered, and the variety of operating environments in which organizations work and compete (i.e., legal and regulatory context, labor market realities, community and societal expectations/relationships, business cultures and norms). Increasing competitive pressures, globalization, rapid advances in product technologies, changing demographics in the customer bases both within domestic markets and across borders, and shifts in business/government relationships all signal a need to measure an organization's response and impact on business diversity.

What sites must be visited along the measurement journey?

Calculating diversity's return-on-investment requires asking key questions and performing key tasks along the way. To achieve a successful result, measuring diversity return-on-investment (DROI) requires a systematic approach that takes into account both costs and benefits. The Hubbard Diversity ROI Analysis Model provides a step-by-step approach that keeps the process manageable so users can tackle one issue at a time.

How to Calculate Diversity ROI

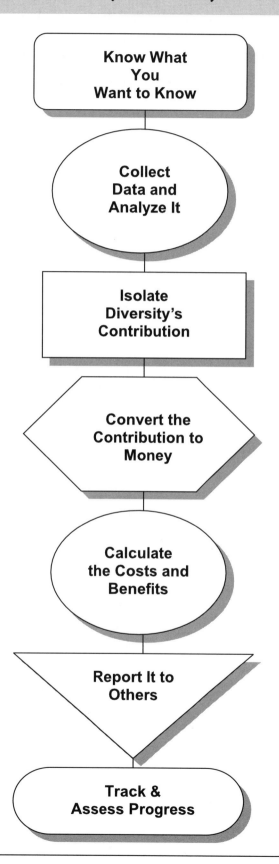

Know What
You
Want to Know

Collect
Data and
Analyze It

Isolate
Diversity's
Contribution

Convert the
Contribution to
Money

Calculate
the Costs and
Benefits

Report It to
Others

Track &
Assess Progress

The model also emphasizes that this is a logical, systematic process, which flows from one step to another. Applying the model provides consistency from one DROI calculation to another. In essence, it suggests that the major aspects of diversity measurement you need to address include:

- Knowing what you want to know
- Collecting data and analyzing it
- Isolating diversity's contribution
- Converting the contribution to money
- Calculating the costs and benefits
- Reporting it to others
- Tracking and assessing progress

Step 1: Know What You Want To Know

Conducting a diversity return-on-investment study requires that you clearly identify what you want to know as a result of implementing the study. This should be based upon, at bare minimum, the identification of a business problem or opportunity related to the organization's key business strategy. Second, you should be prepared to list a series of research questions you would like answered or hypotheses you would like to test. These questions may include things such as "In what racial categories do we have the most turnover?", "What diverse customer markets are not utilizing our products or services?", "How can we improve the idea and solution generation (creative) process using current

cross-functional teams to improve operational performance?",
etc.

While planning ways to address these research questions
and ideas, it may be helpful to *begin with the end in mind.*
That is, think of what will appear on your research report,
create placeholders for them, and then generate the
questions or hypotheses that must be answered in order for
data to show up on the report as results. The final step in
this phase is to summarize the questions you would like
answered and formulate diversity measurement study
objectives that will guide your work. Once this is done, you
are ready to consider the appropriate data collection methods
and develop your data collection plan.

Step 2: Collect Data And Analyze It

Data collection is central to the diversity return-on-investment
(DROI) process. In some situations, post-DROI study data
are collected and compared to pre-study situations, control
group differences, and expectations. Both hard data,
representing output, quality, cost, time and frequency; and
soft data, including work habits, work climate, and attitudes
are collected. Data are collected using a variety of methods
including but not limited to:

- Follow-up surveys
- Post-study interviews

- Focus groups
- Short term pilot project assignments
- Action plans
- Performance contracts (agreements to produce certain levels of results)
- Performance monitoring (reports and other literature reviews)
- Etc.

The important challenge in the data collection phase is to select the method or methods appropriate for the organizational setting and within the time and budget constraints of the organization. During this phase, you will identify the data collection processes and specific metrics to use, create the appropriate evaluation instruments, and apply an organizational change methodology such as the Hubbard Diversity 9-S Framework (Shared Vision, Shared Values, Standards, Strategy, Structure, Systems, Style, Skills and Staff).

Step 3: Isolate Diversity's Contribution

An often-overlooked issue in most diversity assessments or evaluation studies is the process of isolating the effects of diversity. In this step of the process, specific strategies are explored, which determine the amount of output performance directly related to the diversity initiative. This step is essential because there are many factors that will influence performance data after the diversity initiative. The result is increased accuracy and credibility of the DROI calculation. The following strategies have been utilized by organizations to tackle this important issue:

- Control groups
- Trend lines
- Forecasting model
- Participant estimates
- Supervisor of participant estimates
- Senior management estimates
- Expert estimates
- Subordinate's estimates (those who work for the participants)
- Identifying other influencing factors
- Customer inputs

Collectively, these strategies provide a comprehensive set of tools to tackle the important and critical issue of isolating the effects of diversity initiatives.

Calculating and isolating diversity's return-on-investment will require an analysis of operational and other business processes to isolate the specific areas where diversity can be applied to improve business performance. One tool to analyze operational processes is the "S-I-P-O-C Chain". This analysis tool allows you to break down operational processes and view them in terms of the way business is done from

Supplier to *Input* to *Process* to *Output* to *Customer*. Once all contributing factors have been identified and their contributions calculated you would be ready to convert the contribution to money.

Step 4: Convert The Contribution To Money

To calculate the diversity return-on-investment, data collected in a DROI evaluation study are converted to monetary values and are compared to the diversity initiative costs. This requires a value to be placed on each unit of data connected with the initiative. There are at least ten different strategies available to convert data to monetary values. The specific strategy selected usually depends on the type of data and the initiative under analysis:

- **Output data** are converted to profit contribution or cost saving. In this strategy, output increases are converted to monetary value based on their unit contribution to profit or the unit of cost reduction.

- The **cost of quality** is calculated and quality improvements are directly converted to cost savings.

- For diversity initiatives where employee time is saved, the **participant's wages and benefits** are used for the value of time. Because a variety of programs focus on improving the time required to complete projects, processes, or daily activities, the value of time becomes an important and critical issue.

How to Calculate Diversity ROI

- **Historical costs** are used when they are available for a specific variable. In this case, organizational cost data are utilized to establish the specific value of an improvement.

- When available, **internal and external experts** may be used to estimate a value for an improvement. In this situation, the credibility of the estimate hinges on the expertise and reputation of the individual.

- **External databases** are sometimes available to estimate the value or cost of data items. Research, government, and industry databases can provide important information for these values. The difficulty lies in finding a specific database related to the diversity initiative under analysis.

- **Participants** estimate the value of the data item. For this approach to be effective, participants must be capable of providing a value for the improvement.

- **Supervisors of participants** provide estimates when they are both willing and capable of assigning values to the improvement. This approach is especially useful when participants are not fully capable of providing this input or in situations where supervisors need to confirm or adjust the participant's estimate.

- **Senior management** may provide estimates on the values of an improvement. This approach is particularly helpful to establish values for performance measures that are very important to senior management.

- **Diversity staff** estimates may be used to determine a value of an output data item. In these cases, it is essential for the estimates to be provided on an unbiased basis.

Step 4 in the Hubbard Diversity Return-on-investment Analysis Model is very important and is absolutely necessary for determining the monetary benefits from a diversity initiative. The process is challenging, particularly with soft data, but can be methodologically accomplished using one or more of these strategies.

Step 5: Calculate the Costs and Benefits

Calculating the Diversity Initiative Costs

To successfully calculate DROI, both cost and benefits must be tracked and calculated in the process. The first part of the equation on a cost/benefit analysis is the diversity initiative costs. Tabulating the costs involves monitoring or developing all of the related costs of the diversity initiative targeted for the DROI calculation. Among the cost components that should be included are:

- The cost to design and develop the diversity initiative, possibly prorated over the expected life of the initiative;
- The cost of any materials and external staff resources utilized;
- The costs of any facilities, travel, lodging, etc.

How to Calculate Diversity ROI

- Salaries, plus employee benefits of the employee's involved;
- Administrative and overhead costs allocated in some way.

Calculating the Diversity Return on Investment

The diversity return-on-investment is calculated using the initiative's benefits and costs. The benefit/cost ratio (BCR) is the initiative benefits divided by cost. In formula form it is:

BCR = Diversity Initiative Benefits / Diversity Initiative Costs

Sometimes the ratio is stated as a cost-to-benefit ratio, although the formula is the same as BCR.

The diversity return on investment calculation uses the net benefits of the diversity initiative divided by the initiative costs. The net benefits are the diversity initiative benefits minus the costs. As a formula, it is stated as:

DROI% = (Net Diversity Initiative Benefits / Initiative Costs)*100

In other words, the DROI formula is calculated as:

$$\frac{\text{Diversity Benefits} - \text{Initiative Costs}}{\text{Initiative Cost}} \times 100$$

This is the same basic formula used in evaluating other investments where the ROI is traditionally reported as earnings divided by investment. The DROI from some diversity initiatives is often high. DROI figures above 450% are not uncommon.

Identifying Intangible Benefits

In addition to tangible, monetary benefits, most diversity initiatives will have intangible, non-monetary benefits. The DROI calculation is based on converting both hard and soft data to monetary values. Intangible benefits include items such as:

- Increased job satisfaction
- Increased organizational commitment
- Improved teamwork
- Reduced conflict
- Etc.

During data analysis, every attempt is made to convert all data to monetary values. All hard data such as output, quality, and time are converted to monetary values. The conversion of soft data is attempted for each data item. However, if the process used for conversion is too subjective or inaccurate, the resulting values can lose credibility in the process. This data should be listed as an intangible benefit with the appropriate explanation. For some diversity initiatives, intangible, non-monetary benefits are extremely valuable, often carrying as much influence as the hard data items.

Step 6: Report It to Others

Next, it is critical that you have an organized communications plan to let others know the progress and challenges being addressed by diversity initiatives. During the development cycle of the communications plan, it is important to identify communication vehicles to use, how and when the report will be created, when it will be delivered and how to evaluate its implementation.

Step 7: Track and Assess Progress

Finally, in order to maintain any gains made or benefits from lessons learned during the process, you must make plans to track and assess the effectiveness of your diversity initiatives over time.

Your Challenge

In summary, the implementation of your diversity return-on-investment study is very critical to the success of the organization and the credibility and survival of the diversity profession. In order to be taken seriously, diversity organizations must become adept at measuring diversity results that tie diversity to the organization's bottom-line objectives. By using a systematic, logical, planned approach, the diversity return-on-investment process is one of the organization's best investments in improved performance!

Step 1 – Know What You Want To Know

Step 1 - Know What You Want To Know

Introduction

In order to get your diversity measurement study off to a successful start, it is critical that you "know what you would like to know". There are many different aspects of the organization where you could analyze the impact of diversity initiatives on bottom-line goals and objectives. Selecting the right initiative or program to analyze requires thoughtful consideration of issues such as:

➢ Importance of the initiative in meeting strategic business goals
➢ Linkage of the initiative to cultural, operational, performance, and productivity issues
➢ Adequacy of the needs assessment
➢ Visibility of the initiative
➢ Size of the target audience
➢ Cost of the initiative
➢ Senior management request

How to Calculate Diversity ROI

Therefore, it is imperative that your approach is focused and strategic. It must examine the key impact areas that link to organizational goals and objectives. The following considerations will help clarify what you want to know.

Identify a Business Problem Related to the Organization's Strategy

Diversity departments and diversity initiatives do not operate in a vacuum. The business issues above, below, and around them are usually the goals objectives that the diversity organization must support and link with. To effectively know what you want to know, your diversity measurement approach must connect with the needs of the business.

Generally, measurement research projects are undertaken for one of two reasons: 1) to solve a problem, or 2) to take advantage of an opportunity. When diversity can be used to help the organization solve a real business problem such as hiring or retaining a diverse workforce, improving functional integration, blending cultures during an acquisition or merger, it adds value. Diversity also contributes by taking advantage of opportunities such as penetrating new diverse markets, improving diverse customer satisfaction, etc. This presents a strong business case and supports the organization's goals and objectives.

Definitions

The following definitions may be helpful as you work through the DROI process:

Business unit: A logical sub-unit of the larger system. Large corporations can have business units that are as large as other entire companies.

Work processes: A series of steps that transform some input or raw material into a useful product for a customer of the process.

How to Check Organizational Measures

Measuring diversity results requires that you know what organizational measures to connect to. This means that you must check out what to measure. You should:

> ➤ Learn what is measured at the organization, business unit and work process levels
> ➤ Determine if the measures are balanced (that is, do they measure financial, customer, internal business, and learning perspectives, or only financial perspectives?). Linking your diversity measurement studies to a balanced set of measures is a more effective approach.
> ➤ Determine if the diversity team, using its initiatives, can affect the measure directly.

How to Calculate Diversity ROI

What to Do If You Can't Affect The Organization's Measures

If the diversity team can't affect the measures, you have two choices. Change the measures you have selected or do not conduct the diversity assessment study. Asking a diversity team to measure or affect organizational measures that are out of their control will eventually weaken or destroy the team's motivation.

Application Exercise

What to Do Next

1. Review your organization's goals and strategic business objectives.
2. Record these goals and measures using the worksheet on the following page. Note: Do not create any goals. Just record those measures that someone decided were important enough to track for your organization.
3. Place a check mark next to those that the diversity team can affect.

How To Calculate Diversity Return on Investment

Check Your Work on the Following Page

How to Check Your Work

➢ Does your list contain goals and measures for the entire organization?

➢ Does your list contain measures for the levels of the organization above, below, and around the diversity team?

➢ Have you checked the measures that the diversity team can affect?

Note: The information you develop in this chart will be used in a later exercise.

Organizational Measures Worksheet

Level of Measure	Measures	✓
Entire Organization		
Business Unit Measures		

How to Calculate Diversity ROI

Level of Measure	Measures	✓
Departmental Measures		

Formulate Research Questions

After identifying a clear business reason why you want to measure your diversity results and identifying some of the measures to link to, the next step is to "formulate your research questions".

Formulate a research question for the measures you what to use. These might include:

➢ What is the return-on-investment for the sexual harassment and discrimination program we conducted over the last year?

➢ What is the value of the supplier diversity program we set up for our electronics division?

➢ What was the impact of our "Language Exchange" training program on diverse customer complaints and incremental revenue improvement?

➢ What is the value of the Work Style and Conflict Resolution program we are currently conducting?

➢ What on-the-job improvements have been realized since the diversity initiative was put in place? Etc.

The best approach in formulating research questions is to start broad then narrow the focus. Focus on diversity measurement using the organization's strategic business goals and objectives as your guide. The key to formulating the "right" kind of questions is to help solve and prevent business problems as well as improving business operations.

Begin with the End in Mind -- Your Report

Whenever you formulate a research question, remember that its structure directly affects the analysis you can do. Therefore, begin with the end in mind. By creating a preliminary template of the data and results you would like to see at the end of this study, you would be able to develop a roadmap for the type of questions you must have answered.

Create a final figure format of the report you want without the data. This gives you a layout of what your end report will display.

How to Calculate Diversity ROI

Create the Diversity Measurement Study Objectives

In order to create the best diversity measurement study possible, it is critical that you identify clear, well-stated objectives upon which to base your work. If you conduct a survey, for example, what should the survey ask? What information should it collect? You must know the survey's objectives to answer these questions.

Where Do Diversity Measurement Study Objectives Originate?

The objectives of a diversity measurement study can be generated from the following:

- A defined need e.g., a rise in the number of voluntary turnovers among women and people of color, white males, or any underrepresented group
- Reviews of the diversity literature relating to gaps that may exist in organizations
- Focus groups or consensus panels that focus on a particular problem or opportunity related to diversity
- Etc.

An objective is a statement of the diversity measurement study's hoped-for outcomes. An example of three objectives for a diversity cultural audit are shown below:

Sample Objectives for a Diversity Cultural Audit

1. Identify the most common barriers to career development for women and people of color in the organization by level and business unit.

2. Compare the mentoring needs of men and women of color.

3. Identify the cultural competence of all management staff members based upon the cultural competence model created by the diversity organization.

A specific set of objectives like these suggests a survey that asks questions about the following:

Objective 1: Career Barriers

Sample survey questions: Have you encountered barriers related to your personal career development? If so, what are the most common type of barriers encountered.

Objective 2: Mentoring Needs

Sample survey questions: Are you male or female? What racial group do you identify with using the checkboxes below (write in the space provided if the racial group you need want to check is not listed)? What areas would you like support and development in if it could be provided?

Objective 3: Cultural Competence

Sample survey questions: My manager respects the opinions of women as well as those of men. My manager acts on ideas and suggestions equally regardless of the racial background or gender of the employee.

Generating survey questions with rating scales such as these can be accomplished quickly using automated tools such as Survey Pro[tm] and MetricLINK[tm] which will be discussed later.

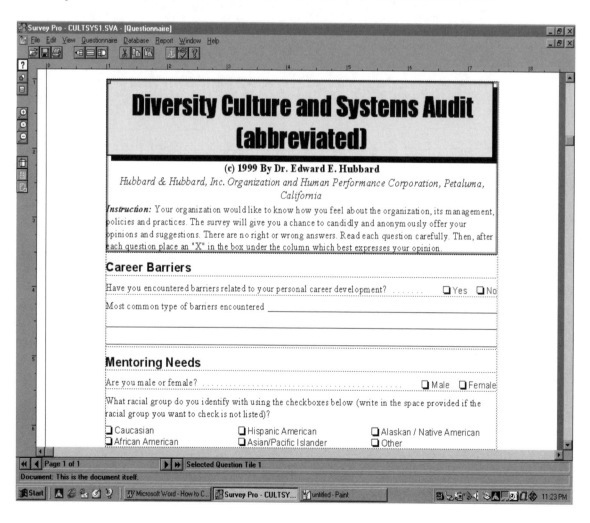

When planning your diversity measurement study objectives, be sure to define all potentially imprecise or ambiguous terms in the objectives. For the objectives above, an imprecise term could have resulted from the use of the term "needs". However, the words "mentoring needs" are used.

Calculating Diversity Return-on-investment (DROI) requires that you clearly "know what you want to know". There's an old saying that states "If you don't know where you are going, any road will take you there". Taking the time to define the specific business reasons why you are conducting the diversity measurement study will provide you with the roadmap for a successful diversity measurement journey.

How to Calculate Diversity ROI

Step 2 – Prepare and Collect Data

Step 2 - Prepare and Collect Data

Introduction

Once you clearly "know what you want to know", you are ready to "prepare and collect data". Just like obtaining a clarity of vision regarding your diversity measurement study direction, the process of collecting data to measure your diversity results comes with its own rules of accomplishment.

Identify Data Collection Measurement Areas

Diversity measurement is easier to understand when you know the specific results for which you are trying to identify measures. This part of the diversity ROI measurement process will help you identify the diversity results you may want to measure.

There are several approaches that may be used to identify the starting point for your diversity measurement efforts. A full range of approaches is discussed in detail in the "***How to Calculate Diversity Return-on-investment***" workshop. In this book, we will utilize one of the measurement point identification options called the "value-added results" method.

Figuring Out What to Measure that is Value-Added

Before we get started identifying diversity value-added measurement points, we'll discuss the concept of a value-added result and how it can help you measure diversity performance.

All diversity measurement will typically flow from either the diverse workforce results, the work processes which the diverse workforce is using to produce these results (approaches that maximize diverse workforce inputs, processes and outputs), or external diverse group contributions and synergies (e.g., diverse supplier and diverse community participation).

Definitions:

Activities are actions that produce results. Attending meetings, talking with people over the phone, participating in a diversity awareness-training program, and solving problems are all activities.

Value-added Results are the products you generate from the activities. They are the diversity-related contributions that add value to the organization and result from the activities. For example, attending diversity awareness training can produce the result: "diversity competent people who are aware of the negative impact of prejudice on productivity levels".

There are a number of reasons why you would use value-added results as a starting point for diversity performance measurement. These reasons include the following:

> **It takes less time.** Agreeing on the results you produce takes less time than agreeing on the best activities to achieve the result. While there can be many ways to achieve the end result, the diverse work team will usually agree more quickly on the "end" and less quickly on the "means".

> **Collecting feedback data is less costly.** Evaluating activities requires that someone is there to watch the activities happen. Evaluating the results of the activities can be done simply by looking at the result.

> **It focuses on what is really important.** Measuring activity places more importance on the activity than on the results of the activity. Unless what you want is activity, focus on measuring diversity results that add value.

Other ways to describe value-added results are:
- Output of the work
- Value-added contributions
- End results

- Products
- Accomplishments

Below, you will find a few examples of activities and categories that are **_not_** value-added results. You can use categories to organize groups of diversity results, but alone, these categories do not describe diverse workforce outputs, end results, products or accomplishments.

Non-Value-Added Activities	Non-Value-Added Categories
■ Diversity Training	■ Profitability
■ Diversity Marketing	■ Quality
■ Diversity Strategic Planning	■ Productivity
■ Cost Reduction	■ Safety
■ Innovating	■ People
■ Process Improvement	■ Teamwork
	■ Service

Examples of Value-added Results

This table lists a few examples of diversity value-added results.

Examples of Diversity Value-added Results
■ Productive diverse work teams
■ More diversity skilled executives
■ Increased diverse customer market sales opportunities
■ Qualified women and minority new-hire candidates
■ Solved diverse customer problems
■ Productive collaborations
■ Continued/increased funding for diversity initiatives
■ Diversity-friendly policies, procedures, and systems to support the organization's direction
■ Solutions to problems
■ Reduced absenteeism in women and people of color employee groups
■ Reduced turnover rate for women and people of color
■ Reduced sexual harassment complaints
■ Reduced lost time accidents among women and people of color
■ Increased ideas per employee
■ Increased unit production performance during a merger and acquisition period
■ Dollar revenue generated
■ Profit from accounts

How to Calculate Diversity ROI

Examples of Diversity Value-added Results

- Delivered products
- Diversity strategic plans
- Diversity competent employees

Use a *noun* as the focus of the result statement. This helps to direct your attention towards the result, and away from the activity that produces the result. Notice the italicized *nouns* in each of these examples:

- ➤ *Techniques* for improving diverse customer markets
- ➤ *Improvements* in diverse work team collaboration
- ➤ Motivated and productive *employees*
- ➤ Increased *diversity friendly policies*

Use adjectives or prepositional phrases to modify the noun if they add clarity or indicate the intent of the result. Notice the italicized adjectives or prepositional phrases in each of these examples:

- ➤ Techniques for *improving diverse customer markets*
- ➤ Improvements *in diverse work team collaboration*
- ➤ *Motivated and productive* employees
- ➤ *Increased* diversity friendly policies
- ➤ *Integrated* diversity strategic plans

Tips for writing value-added results

Do not use a verb as the focus of the result statement. Verbs in the past tense describe a completed activity. Remember, the end of an activity is not necessarily a value-added result.

Use	Avoid
Diversity competent employees	Diversity training classes completed
Women and minority new-hires	Women and minorities recruited
Increased diversity-friendly policies	Diversity-friendly policies written

One activity that is prevalent among diversity initiatives is diversity awareness training. Because "training" is an activity, you'll need to identify the value-added result by asking, "What is left behind after I successfully conduct the diversity awareness training?"

Depending on the situation, you might answer "classes conducted" or "diversity competent employees." We are looking for the value-added result; therefore the best answer would be "diversity competent employees." Classes don't add value, but diversity competent employees are a valuable addition to the organization.

Practice Exercise

What to Do Next

To help you understand the idea of value-added results, here is a chance to practice identifying them.

Read the list below and check those items that you feel fit the definition of a value-added result. You'll find the answers on the next page.

	Item	Result?
1	Increased profitability	❑
2	Evaluating diversity recruiting	❑
3	Diverse work team meetings held	❑
4	Recommendations	❑
5	Productive employees	❑
6	Diverse work group problem solving	❑
7	Improvements in work processes	❑
8	Giving positive feedback	❑

Now that you understand the concept of a value-added result, we can turn our attention to the "identifying value-added results" measurement point method.

**How To Calculate Diversity
Return on Investment**

**Check Your Work on the
Following Page**

How to Check Your Work

Compare your answers to those below. Verbs usually indicate activities. Nouns usually indicate results.

	Item	Result?
1	Increased profitability	✓
2	Evaluating diversity recruiting	
3	Diverse work team meetings held	
4	Recommendations	✓
5	Productive employees	✓
6	Diverse work group problem solving	
7	Improvements in work processes	✓
8	Giving positive feedback	

Diversity Value-added Results Method

This technique works best when the diversity organization's measurement study is focused on identifying value-added improvements in measurable goals such as:

➢ Increasing retention rates of women and people of color

➢ Improving diversity climate

➢ Improving the diversity friendliness of policies, procedures, and systems

How to Calculate Diversity ROI

➤ Assessing the impact of diversity training on performance improvement.

➤ Etc.

In each case, the goal is one that can be measured with numbers and the diversity organization or diverse work group is supposed to help move the numbers in the right direction.

It is important to keep the big picture in mind as you start this process. That is, we are not measuring diversity for diversity sake. It is attached to the context of business. You must examine the results that support the achievement of organizational objectives. This can be accomplished by the following:

1. Review the business issues, research questions and diversity measurement objectives you generated in the "know what you want to know step".

2. Next, review the organizational issues, questions or objectives you are to improve and decide if the diversity initiative can affect them.

3. If the diversity initiative can affect these measurement areas, answer the question, "What value-added result does the diversity initiative produce that can help the organization achieve its goal?"

4. Describe these results as value-added and add them to the list of results you will measure.

Example of diversity results which support organizational goals

Many organizations are striving to become an "Employer of Choice" or appear on the "100 Best Companies to Work For" list. From a diversity standpoint, this business issue is related to a number of areas in which diversity can have an impact. These areas include:

> The recruitment of people of difference (women, people of color, sexual orientation, physical ability, educational discipline, etc.)
> The retention of people of difference
> Reducing the source costs for acquiring these diverse workforce resources
> Creating the training and promotional opportunities for people of difference
> Pay issues related to people of difference (function, level, race, educational background, sexual orientation, physical ability, etc.)

Examining these organizational goals, they can be measured in dollars, numbers, percentages, and anecdotal data. For example, diversity recruitment and retention can be measured in this manner.

The first two steps above state that you should examine the business issues and decide if the diversity initiative can affect these issues, research questions, and diversity measurement objectives. The answer is "yes." Because your diversity organization or diverse work team can work collaboratively with the staffing and recruitment department to improve recruitment and retention systems and processes, you can affect costs, numbers, percentages and anecdotal data in this area.

The next step says to answer the question, "What value-added results does the diversity initiative produce which can help the organization achieve its goals?" In this case the answer is:

➤ Increased people of difference as new hires
➤ Improved retention of skilled employees
➤ Reduced diversity recruitment source costs
➤ Increased promotion-ready people of difference
➤ Reduced pay disparities among people of difference and majority groups

Reviewing Historical Data

Another alternative for identifying diversity measurement areas is reviewing historical data. Data are available in every organization to measure performance. Monitoring performance data enables you to measure diversity results in terms of output, quality, costs, and time. In determining the use of data in the measuring diversity results study, the first consideration should be existing databases and reports. In most organizations, performance data suitable for measuring improvements from a diversity initiative are available. If not, additional record-keeping systems will have to be developed for data collection, measurement, and analysis.

At this point, as with many other points in the process, the question of economics enters. Is it economical to develop the record-keeping system necessary to evaluate a diversity initiative? If the costs are greater than the expected return for the entire program, then it is meaningless to develop them.

Using Current Measures

When using current measures, be sure they are appropriate to the area you want to study. Performance measures should be thoroughly researched to identify those that are related to the proposed objectives of the diversity initiative. Frequently, an organization will have several performance measures related to the same item. For example, if the diversity organization works with the operations department to improve the efficiency of a production unit, it might start by analyzing diverse work styles. The impact of this could be measured in a variety of ways:

- The number of units produced per hour
- The number of on-schedule production units
- The percent of utilization of the new work style
- The percentage of work group downtime due to conflict
- The labor cost per unit of production
- The overtime required per piece of production, and
- The total unit cost

Each of these, in its own way, measures the efficiency of the production unit. All related measures should be reviewed to determine those most relevant to the diversity initiative.

Convert Current Measures to Usable Ones

Occasionally, existing performance measures are integrated with other data, and it may be difficult to keep them isolated from unrelated data. In this situation, all existing related measures should be extracted and re-tabulated to be more appropriate for comparison in the evaluation.

At times, conversion factors may be necessary. For example, the average number of new recruits per month may be presented regularly in the performance measures for the staffing department. In addition, the cost of generating new recruits per recruiter is also presented. However in the evaluation of the impact of a diversity initiative, the "average cost of a diverse hire" is needed. This will require at least two existing performance records to develop the data necessary for comparison (the average number and the cost data).

Develop A Data Collection Plan for Performance Data

A data collection plan defines when, by whom, and where the data are collected. This plan should contain provisions for the evaluator to secure copies of performance reports in a timely manner so that the items can be recorded and are available for analysis.

Developing New Measures

In some cases, data are not available for the information needed to measure the effectiveness of a diversity initiative's impact. The Diversity Department must work with the appropriate department to develop record-keeping systems, if this is economically feasible. In one organization, a new employee orientation program was implemented on a company-wide basis for new hires from diverse backgrounds.

How to Calculate Diversity ROI

Several feedback measures were planned, including early turnover (known as survival and loss rates)-representing the percentage of people of difference who left the company in the first six months of their employment. At the time of the program's inception, this measure was not available. When the program was implemented, the organization had to begin collecting early turnover figures for comparison.

Typical Questions When Creating New Measures
■ Which department will develop the measurement system?
■ Who will record and monitor the data?
■ Where will the information be recorded?
■ How often will you collect data?

These questions will usually involve other departments or a management decision that extends beyond the scope of the Diversity Department. Possibly the administration division, the HR Department, or Information Technology Department will be instrumental in helping determine if new measures are needed and if so, how they will be collected.

Hubbard & Hubbard, Inc.'s Diversity Measurement and Productivity Institute (DM&P) conducts a two-day workshop entitled: "**Measuring Diversity Results**" which concentrates on, among other things, teaching participants how to create new diversity measures, processes and systems to support their initiatives. It is designed to give you a foundation upon which to build your diversity measurement strategies using your specific company's data in class. This will enable you to use it immediately upon your return.

Application Exercise

Identify your organization's diversity value-added results that support the organizational measures you identified earlier using the **_Organizational Measures Worksheet_**.

What to Do Next

- Refer to the Organizational Measures Worksheet in this book (see index for page number), make a copy of it and place it next to this page for easy reference. *Note: Permission to copy this chart is limited to this page only.*
- For those measures that the diversity initiative can affect, identify what the Diversity organization or work team can produce that will affect each measure.
- Define these products as value-added results and write them on the worksheet provided on the next page.

How to Calculate Diversity ROI

Your Diversity Initiative's Value-added Results which

Support Organizational Measures

Value-Added Results

How To Calculate Diversity
Return on Investment

Check Your Work on the
Following Page

How to Check Your Work

Answer these questions:

> ➢ Can the diversity initiative influence these measures?
>
> ➢ Will these products lead to an improvement in the organization's measures?
>
> ➢ Are the products written as value-added with a noun as the focus?

Conducting Interviews

An often used and very helpful data collection method is the interview, although it is not used as frequently as questionnaires. Interviews can be conducted by a variety of people including the diversity staff, other department members and outside third parties. Interviews can secure data not available in performance records, or data that is difficult to obtain through written responses or observations. Also, interviews can uncover success stories that can be useful in communicating results that illustrate diversity's contribution to the strategic business objectives of the organization.

Interviewees may be reluctant to describe their results in a questionnaire but will volunteer the information to a skillful interviewer who uses probing techniques. A major disadvantage of the interview is that it is time-consuming. It also requires training or preparing interviewers to ensure that the process is consistent.

Types of Interviews

Interviews usually fall into two basic categories: (1) structured and (2) unstructured. A structured interview is much like a questionnaire. Specific questions are asked with little room to deviate from the desired responses. The primary advantages of the structured interview over the questionnaire are that the interview process can ensure that the questionnaire is completely filled out and the interviewer understands the responses supplied by the participant.

The unstructured interview allows you to probe for additional information. This type of interview uses a few general questions, which can lead into more detailed information as important data are uncovered. The interviewer must be skilled in the probing process.

Typical Probing Questions
Can you explain that in more detail?
Can you give an example of what you are saying?
Can you explain the difficulty that you say you encountered?

Interview Guidelines

The design steps for an interview are similar to the process you would use for a questionnaire. A brief summary of the key issues with interviews is outlined here.

Develop questions to be asked. Once a decision has been made about the type of interview, specific questions need to be developed. Questions should be brief, precise and designed for easy response.

Try out the interview. The interview should be tested on a small group of people in the target population. If possible, the interviews should be conducted as part of a trial run or pilot test of your diversity initiative. The responses should be analyzed and the interview questions revised based upon the reaction and responses received during the test.

Train the interviewers. The interviewer should have the appropriate skills, including active listening, probing question skills, and the ability to collect and summarize data into meaningful forms.

Give clear instructions to the participant. The participant should understand the purpose of the interview and know what will be done with the information. Expectations, conditions, and the rules of the interview should be thoroughly discussed. For example, the participant should know if the statements will be kept confidential. If the participant is nervous during the interview and develops signs of anxiety, he or she should be made to feel at ease.

Administer the interview according to a scheduled plan. As with the other evaluation instruments, interviews need to be conducted according to a predetermined plan. The timing of the interview, the person who conducts the interview, and the place of the interview are all issues that become relevant when developing an interview plan. For a large number of participants, a sampling plan may be necessary to save time and reduce evaluation cost.

Conduct Focus Groups

Focus groups are an extension of the interview process. They are particularly helpful when in-depth feedback is needed on the impact of diversity initiatives. Focus groups involve small group discussions conducted by an experienced facilitator. It is designed to solicit qualitative judgments on a planned topic or issue. Group members are all required to provide their input, as individual input builds on group input.

When compared with questionnaires, surveys, tests, or interviews, a focus group strategy has several advantages. The basic premise for using focus groups is that when quality judgment are subjective, several individual judgments about the effectiveness of a diversity initiative is better than one. The group process, where participants often motivate each other, is a great method for generating new ideas and hypotheses. It is inexpensive and can be quickly planned and conducted. Its flexibility makes it possible to explore a diversity initiative's unexpected outcomes or applications.

Focus groups are particularly helpful when qualitative information is needed about the success of a diversity initiative. It provides you with the anecdotal data to support the trends and other quantitative data you may have generated.

Guidelines for Focus Groups

While there are no set rules on how to use focus groups for evaluation purposes, some general guidelines might help you in their use:

Ensure that management buys into the focus group process. Some members of management may not be familiar with the focus group technique. Managers may need to understand focus groups and their advantages. This should help raise their level of confidence in the information obtained from these sessions.

How to Calculate Diversity ROI

Plan topics, questions, and strategies carefully. As with any evaluation instrument, planning is key. The specific topics, questions, and issues to be discussed must be carefully planned and sequenced. This enhances the comparison of results from one group with another and ensures that the group process is effective and stays on track.

Keep the group size small. While there is no magic group size, a range of 6 to 12 seems to be appropriate for most focus group applications. A group has to be large enough to ensure different points of view, but small enough to give every participant a chance to talk freely and exchange comments.

Ensure that there is a representative sample of the target population. It is important for the group to be stratified appropriately so that the participants represent the target population. The group should be homogeneous in experience rank, influence in the organization and reflect those affected by the diversity initiative.

Insist on facilitators who have appropriate expertise. The success of the focus group rests with the facilitator who must be skilled in the focus group process. Facilitators must know how to control aggressive members of the group and diffuse the input from those who want to dominate the group. Also, facilitators must be able to create an environment in which participants feel comfortable enough to offer comments freely and openly. Because of this, some organizations use external facilitators.

In summary, focus groups are an inexpensive and quick way to determine the strengths and weaknesses of the diversity initiatives you may implement. However, for complete evaluation, focus group information should be combined with other evaluation data from other instruments to gain a holistic picture of your results.

Analyzing Your Diversity Change Efforts using the Hubbard Diversity 9-S Framework

The Hubbard Diversity 9-S Framework will help you holistically examine your diversity change efforts to ensure alignment with key organizational variables. The measurements serve as lenses for viewing and measuring diversity initiative's effectiveness.

As you prepare and collect data for your diversity study, consider whether your diversity initiative has organizational support in each of the Diversity 9-S Framework areas. When this support **is not** present, the diversity initiative tends to be less successful. When it is present, the initiative is reinforced with a powerful, integrated, strategic force for producing a successful culture change. An example of the framework is shown below.

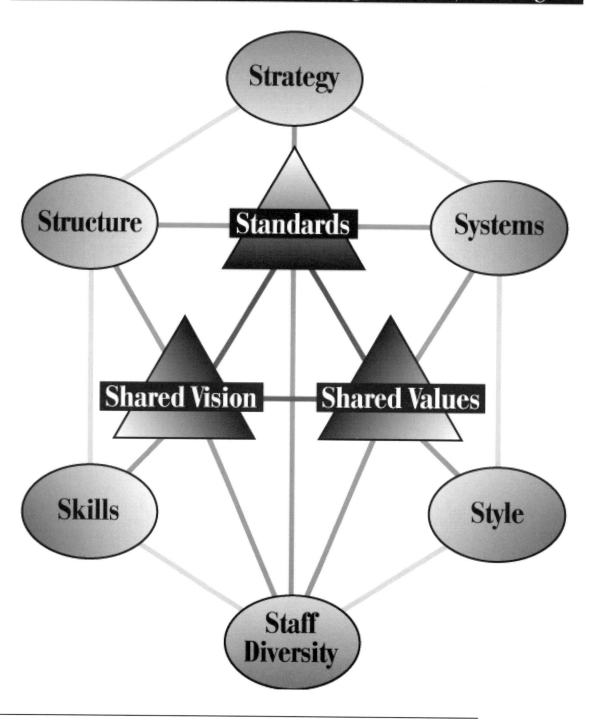

Diversity 9-S Framework for Organizational Change

Strategy

Structure　Standards　Systems

Shared Vision　Shared Values

Skills　Style

Staff Diversity

Let's take a look at the Diversity 9-S Framework elements and how they are defined.

Shared Vision

This element suggests a mutually derived strategic direction among employees, management, and the organization's customers. It reflects the organization's aspirations, purpose, goals, and objectives. It is represented by a visual image of a desired future for the organization to meet the strategic needs of its stakeholders.

When measuring this dimension of the Diversity 9-S Framework, it is important to examine:

- The clarity of the diversity vision for the organization and its key stakeholders
- The presence of an organizational visual image illustrating the desired future state in pictures, images, sounds, and feelings that will be in place once this future state is achieved
- How thoroughly diversity initiatives are being supported, and what can be done to further the achievement of the diversity vision

Shared Values

This element requires a re-examination of organizational values and culture or the "guiding and daily beliefs." It offers an opportunity to interpret values and identity and bridge any gaps between espoused values and individual behavior. This requires an investment of time and resources.

Top management must make a commitment to ensure that values related to diversity are clearly understood and practiced by all. If the principle values of leveraging diversity are in place and operating, they will be seen in what people do, not what's written in a brochure about your culture.

When measuring this element of the Diversity 9-S Framework, it is important to examine:

- The decisions and policies that illustrate these values
- The rewards for honoring these values and how they relate to stated diversity initiatives
- The personal values and organizational actions that illustrate their use in day-to-day business operations

Standards

This element includes concise, measurable success factors that apply to all aspects of the organizational framework. It provides consistent feedback on how well the organization is meeting its diversity commitments to all stakeholders during and after the transition and change process. The diversity standards dimension is the benchmark of the effort.

Organization systems that are highly accountable require that each system be supported by critical success factors that reflect changes to the organization and its customers.

When measuring this dimension of the Diversity 9-S Framework, it is important to examine:

- The need for measurement tracking systems
- Hard and soft diversity measures of performance. A visible reward system to support the achievement of these measures
- Whether best practices have been identified and benchmarked
- "Report card" and/or "mental model" diversity measures that assess effectiveness at the activity, process, outcome, and value-added levels

Strategy

This element includes tactics, plans and integrating mechanisms for business objectives, as well as plans and programs that relate to valuing and leveraging diversity. An organization's marketing, financial and operations strategies have direct linkages to the full utilization of its human resources.

Effectively utilizing this element in a diversity change effort requires that each organization have a "human capital plan" that is every bit as strategic as the allocation of its business capital. Opportunities abound for organizations that make explicit, concrete connections between the goals of the organization and the effective management of diverse workforce resources.

When measuring this dimension of the Diversity 9-S Framework, it is important to identify and examine:

- Diversity work practices that leverage the talents and skills of diverse work teams
- The groups that influence strategy formulation and monitoring the requirements for diverse workforce representation and input
- Formal business strategies to determine if they are built to capitalize on diverse workforce resources to meet competitive and other organizational needs

Structure

This element makes certain that the proper organization structural framework is in place to support an inclusive work environment. Are new reporting relationship structures needed within the organization to convey the sense of urgency, accountability, and importance for utilizing the talents of the diverse workforce?

Are new task forces, advisory committees, or self-directed teams needed to address and direct attention to diversity issues? Changes in the organization chart and its structure send a loud message about who and what are important.

When measuring this dimension of the Diversity 9-S Framework, it is important to examine:

- Whether operational and team structures are designed to support diversity

- Whether integrating mechanisms exist for problem solving and information sharing using workforce diversity.

- Are diverse or cross–functional work teams and individuals from all across the organization able to have access and work among and within those levels? Are structural barriers removed (e.g., communication, promotional, etc.)

Systems

This element includes such organizational components as recruitment and hiring practices, training and development policies, promotion and succession rules, performance appraisal regulations, and compensation practices. Each must be examined to determine congruency with the organization's diversity strategies.

In essence, all policies, practices, rules, regulations, and procedures that employees follow to perform job-related duties must be examined for possible change.

How to Calculate Diversity ROI

When measuring this dimension of the Diversity 9-S
Framework, it is important to examine:

- How policies, procedures, rules, and regulations are
  designed to support the diversity change effort
- Whether different modes of decision-making,
  problem solving, and communication are used to
  manage and leverage diversity.

Skills

This element represents the talents and abilities of the
workforce that can give an organization its competitive
advantage. The relationship between the skills an
organization possesses in managing and leveraging diversity
and the bottom-line gains achieved go hand-in-hand.

Leveraging the rich talents of a diverse work group can add
exponentially to an organization's quality of output and
productivity. Employee and management skills for working in
a diverse work environment must be valued as a competitive
organizational asset.

When measuring this dimension of the Diversity 9-S
Framework, it is important to examine:

- Whether core diversity competencies are in place
  and evaluated for all levels of employees
- Whether Level 3 training evaluation (skill transfer)
  methods are in place and fully utilized to gauge

whether participants are applying their diversity awareness. And are participants using skills for inclusion while carrying out their job

Style

This element includes the day-to-day management and leadership behavior that ultimately creates the climate of the organization (in other words, "what it's like to work here"). Style represents a major force that models the priorities of the organization in everyday behavior. It can be seen in how management and leaders of the organization facilitate the process of organizational performance. It is reflected in how people are treated and the level of acceptance of differences that prevails.

The organization's style must reflect a strong sensitivity and practice for effectively utilizing a diverse workforce in pursuit of organizational objectives.

When measuring this dimension of the Diversity 9-S Framework, it is important to examine:

- The degree to which prevailing managerial practices and styles are supportive of workforce diversity
- How current cultural practices support diversity (rites, mentoring, rituals, ceremony)

How to Calculate Diversity ROI

Staff

This element includes a profile of the employee body or the types of people residing (and where) in the organization. Information about the organization's primary and secondary dimensions of diversity must be known and leveraged.

A typical misconception is that many more women and minorities reside in the organization across functions and at higher levels. Staying informed of the organization's workforce statistics, as well as current and future labor needs, will assist everyone in responding to the challenges of a diverse organizational and customer marketplace.

When measuring this dimension of the Diversity 9-S Framework, it is important to examine:

- Whether the employee base reflects the target diversity mix at all levels
- What groups are under-represented
- What staffing requirements are needed to meet national or global competitive needs
- How your employee mix matches your customer mix

Hubbard & Hubbard, Inc. provides a complete Diversity 9-S Framework Audit package to help organizations examine each of the Diversity 9-S Framework areas in detail. It is designed to take the guesswork out of evaluating and interpreting the data gathered from each dimension.

Once you have completed your Diversity 9-S Audit, you are ready to begin crafting a primary data collection instrument.

Checklist of Typical Survey Tasks

The following information provides a checklist of things to consider when you are ready to tackle the task of surveying your organization. Perhaps the most important issue to consider when completing these tasks is deciding whether to create or purchase an evaluation instrument. When reaching this point, it is vital to think about the complexity of the task and the type of data to be collected. At any rate, these steps will provide some standard guidelines for successfully completing the task.

Checklist of Typical Survey Tasks
Identify the Survey's Objectives
■ Conduct focus or consensus groups to identify the needs, goals and objectives
■ Obtain official approval of the objectives
■ Conduct a review of the diversity literature to define terms to be used in the survey and justify theory underlying questions.

Checklist of Typical Survey Tasks

Design the Survey Approach

- Know alternative research designs and their implementation steps. Or purchase a psychometrically sound survey or hire an expert to create a custom survey.
- Choose a survey design method
- Decide on a sample size and select sample using technically sound sampling methods

Purchase or Prepare the Survey Instrument

- Developing psychometrically sound survey instruments is both a science and an art. You may want to examine what diversity measurement instrumentation already exists that may be close to the objectives of your assessment. There are a variety of survey instruments on the market that may meet your diversity measurement needs. In addition consultation is available to customize survey questions and assist in processing and reporting data. If you plan to create your own survey, the following tips may be helpful
  - ➢ Conduct a literature review
  - ➢ Contact others in your organization who conduct surveys
  - ➢ Adapt some or all of the questions on existing surveys
  - ➢ Prepare a new instrument

Checklist of Typical Survey Tasks

Pilot-test the Instrument

- Obtain permission for the pilot test
- Identify a sample audience for the pilot test
- Analyze the pilot test data
- Revise the instrument to make it final

Administer the Survey

- Hire staff or train staff
- Monitor the quality of the administration
- Send out survey in the mail
- Conduct interview(s)
- Follow-up

Organize the Data

- Code responses
- Consult with programmer to analyze data
- Train the data entry staff
- Enter the data into a computer
- Run a preliminary analysis
- Clean the data
- Prepare a codebook of response issues

How to Calculate Diversity ROI

Checklist of Typical Survey Tasks
Analyze the Data
■ Prepare an analysis plan
■ Review the psychometric properties of the instrument to categorize data
■ Analyze the results of the survey
Report the Data
■ Write the report
■ Have the report reviewed
■ Modify the report based upon the reviews
■ Prepare overheads and other multi-media support tools
■ Present the report orally

The data collection step is usually the most time-consuming of all of the steps and is also the part of the Diversity ROI process that can be the most disruptive to the organization. This step is critical to the success of the Diversity ROI measurement process. It creates the foundation upon which the remaining analysis tasks rest. It is worth the time and effort to thoughtfully and carefully complete each task.

Step 3 – Isolate Diversity's Contribution

Step 3 - Isolate Diversity's Contribution

Introduction

Once you have prepared and collected the data, you are ready to isolate diversity's contribution. This step will help you select a method to isolate diversity's contribution to the organization's goals and objectives. Although there are at least ten (10) different approaches available to accomplish this (such as control groups, trend-line analysis, path analysis, etc.), we will focus on the use of three of them: participant, supervisor, and management estimates.

A Common Diversity Embarrassment

The following situation is repeated often. A significant increase in performance is noted after a major diversity intervention was implemented and the two events appear to be linked. A key manager asks, "How much of this improvement was caused by the diversity initiative?" When this potentially embarrassing question was asked, it is rarely answered with any degree of accuracy and credibility. While the change in performance may be linked to the diversity initiative, other non-diversity factors also have contributed to the improvement.

This chapter explores three useful strategies to isolate the effects of diversity. These strategies are utilized in leading organizations as they attempt to measure the return-on-investment in areas such as diversity, training and development, and the like.

The cause and effect relationship between diversity and performance can be very confusing and difficult to prove, but can be accomplished with an acceptable degree of accuracy. However, is proof the only reason we measure diversity results and performance? The answer is a resounding "NO"!

Diversity and the Double Standard Subterfuge

Diversity is often held to a double standard when it comes to measurement. Disciplines such as Marketing and Finance, for example, are not asked to prove that inflation will be a particular number. The Compensation and Benefits department is not asked to prove that actuarial tables are accurate predictors of exactly when a person will die, yet they base many insurance and retirement benefits on them. Or what about executive retreats with the top management team? Has anyone asked for proof that spending thousands of dollars to host executives (and often their families) for a weekend of golf, relaxation, and a little business has yielded a specific dollar return-on-investment? I am not suggesting that these activities are not important, only that the same yardstick should apply in all places.

Proof is only a minor reason to calculate diversity ROI. A few, more important reasons you should calculate diversity ROI include:

- Assessing progress, urgency, and impact
- Increasing awareness, skill, and productivity
- Improving structures, processes and systems
- Discontinuing or expanding initiatives
- Approving diversity initiatives/projects (if pilots)
- Building a database on diversity performance and results
- Enhancing management and others understanding and support
- Improving measurement skills of the diversity staff
- Achieving corporate, business unit, governmental, non-profit, individual, and community goals

The challenge is to develop one or more specific strategies to isolate the effects of diversity early in the process, usually as part of an evaluation plan. Up-front attention ensures the appropriate strategies will be used with minimum costs and time commitments.

How to Calculate Diversity ROI

Let's take a look at some preliminary considerations.

Preliminary Considerations

Diversity Value Chain Impact

Before presenting the strategies, it may be helpful to consider the chain of impact implied at different stages in the "Diversity Value-Chain" process. Measurable results achieved from a diversity initiative or intervention should be derived from the application of diversity skills and knowledge on the job over a specified period of time after the diversity initiative has been implemented. This on-the-job application of diversity illustrates the notion that it is critical to link diversity to performance as shown below:

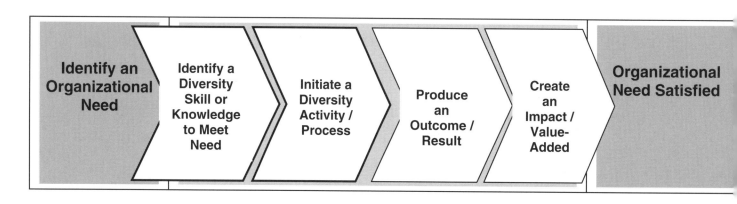

Continuing with this "Diversity Value Chain" logic, successful application of the diversity initiative on the job should stem from participants in the diversity initiative learning and applying diversity knowledge and technologies in a formalized situation to meet a specific organizational goal or objective. Therefore, for an improvement in business results to be realized, this diversity value chain impact implies that measurable on-the-job applications of diversity knowledge & skills are utilized (that is, tasks are performed such as multi-cultural marketing, minority recruitment, bilingual customer service efforts, etc). Without this preliminary evidence, it is difficult to isolate the effects of diversity. In other words, if there is no specific learning or application of diversity strategies and technologies on the job, it is virtually impossible to conclude that the diversity initiative or intervention caused any performance improvements.

In addition, it is vital that measurements are taken throughout the entire diversity value chain. While this requirement is a prerequisite to isolating the effects of diversity, it does not prove that there was a direct connection nor does it pinpoint how much of the improvement was caused by the diversity initiative. It merely shows that without improvements at each stage of the diversity value chain, it is difficult to make a connection between the ultimate outcome and the diversity initiative.

Identifying Other Factors: A First Step

As a first step in isolating diversity's impact on performance, all of the key factors that may have contributed to the performance improvement should be identified. This step communicates to interested parties that other factors may have influenced the results, underscoring that the diversity initiative is not the sole source of improvement. Consequently, the credit for improvement is shared with several possible variables and sources, an approach that is likely to gain the respect of those reviewing the results.

Several potential sources can be used to identify the major influencing variables. For example, if the diversity initiative is designed on request, the client may be able to identify factors that will influence the output variable. Clients will usually be aware of other initiatives or programs that may impact the output.

Participants in the diversity initiative are usually aware of other influences that may have caused performance improvement. After all, it is the impact of their collective efforts that is being monitored and measured. In many situations, they witness previous movements in the performance measures and pinpoint the reasons for changes.

Organization analyst and diversity practitioners who conduct the Needs Analysis are another source for identifying variables that have an impact on results. The needs analysis will usually uncover these influencing variables. Diversity practitioners must analyze these variables while addressing organizational performance issues.

In some situations, supervisors who are involved in or affected by the performance improvement project using diversity may be able to identify variables that influence the performance improvement. This is particularly useful when the primary diversity initiative participants are non-exempt employees who may not be fully aware of the variables that can influence all of the systemic performance elements.

Finally, middle and top management may be able to identify other influences based on their experience and knowledge of the situation. Perhaps they have monitored, examined and analyzed the variables previously. The authority level of these individuals often increases the credibility of the data.

Taking time to focus attention on variables that may have influenced performance brings additional accuracy and credibility to the process. It also moves beyond the scenarios where results are presented with no mention of other influences, a situation that often destroys the credibility of a diversity impact report. It also provides a foundation for some of the strategies described in this toolkit by identifying the variables that must be isolated to show the effects of diversity. Keep in mind that halting the process after this step would leave many unknowns about the actual diversity impact and might leave a negative impression with management and others, since the study may identify variables that management did not previously consider. Therefore, you should go beyond this initial step and use one or more of the strategies discussed in this book that isolate the impact of diversity.

Participant Estimates of Diversity's Impact

An easily implemented method to isolate the impact of diversity is to obtain information directly from the employees involved in the diversity initiative. The effectiveness of this approach rests on the assumption that employees involved in the diversity initiative are capable of determining or estimating how much of a performance improvement is related to the diversity initiative. Because their actions have produced the improvement, participants may have very accurate input on the issue. They should know how much of a change was caused by applying the diversity approaches they learned. Although an estimate, this value will usually have considerable credibility with management because these employees are at the center of the change or improvement.

Let's take a look at an example of one participant's estimations for a particular diversity initiative:

Example of a Participant's Estimation		
Factors that Influenced Improvement	**Percent of Improvement Caused By**	**Confidence Expressed as a Percent**
1. Diversity Multicultural Marketing Program	50%	70%
2. Change in Procedures	10%	80%
3. Adjustment in Standards	10%	50%
4. Revision to Incentive Plan	20%	90%
5. Increased Management Attention	10%	50%
6. Other_____	___%	___%
Total	100%	

Here are some typical questions that must be answered when a participant estimate is considered:

Typical Questions to Answer
<ul><li>What percentage of this improvement can be attributed to the application of diversity skills/knowledge/techniques gained in a diversity training program, from the employee's background and experience, etc.?</li><li>What is the basis for this estimate?</li><li>What confidence do you have in this estimate, expressed as a percent?</li><li>What other factors contributed to this improvement in performance?</li><li>What other individuals or groups could estimate this percentage or determine the amount?</li></ul>

How to Calculate Diversity ROI

Participants who do not provide information on these questions are excluded from the analysis. Also, erroneous, incomplete, and extreme information should be discarded before the analysis. To be conservative, the confidence percentage can be factored into the values. The confidence percentage is actually a reflection of the error in the estimate. Therefore, an 80% confidence level equates to a potential error range of ±20%. With this approach, the level of confidence is multiplied by the estimate using the lower side of the range. In the example, the following process steps explain how this calculation is applied:

- The participant allocates 50% of the improvement to the diversity multicultural marketing program, but is only 70% confident about this estimate

- The confidence percentage is multiplied by the estimate to develop a usable diversity impact factor value of 35%

- The adjusted percentage is then multiplied by the actual amount of the improvement (post-initiative minus pre-initiative value) to isolate the portion attributed to diversity

- The adjusted improvement is now ready for conversion to monetary values and, ultimately used in the diversity return-on-investment calculation

Perhaps an illustration of this process can reveal its effectiveness and acceptability. In a large global organization, the impact of a diversity leadership and mentoring program for new managers was being assessed. Because the decision to calculate the impact of this diversity training was made after the program had been conducted, the control group method was not feasible as a method to isolate the effect of diversity. Also, before the program was implemented, no specified Level 4 (Kirkpatrick Model - business results level) data were identified that were linked to the training program. Consequently, it was difficult to use trend line analysis.

Participants' estimates proved to be the most useful way to estimate the impact. In a detailed follow-up questionnaire, participants were asked a variety of questions regarding the job applications of what was learned from the program. As part of the program, the individuals were asked to develop action plans and implement them, although there was no specific follow-up plan needed. The following series of impact questions were provided with estimations of the diversity impact.

Diversity Impact Questions

- How have you and your job changed as a result of attending this program? (Skills and Knowledge Application)
- What is the impact of these changes in your work unit?

Diversity Impact Questions

(Specific Measures)

- What is the annual value of this change or improvement in your work unit? (Although this is difficult, please make every effort to estimate this value.)

- What is the basis for the estimate provided above? (Please indicate the assumptions you made and the specific calculations you performed to arrive at the value.)

- What confidence do you place in the estimate above? (100%=Certainty, 0%=No Confidence)

- Recognizing that many factors influence output results in addition to this diversity training initiative, please estimate the percent of the improvement that is directly related to this program. (It may be helpful to first identify all the other factors and then provide an estimate of the diversity factor.)

Although these questions are challenging, when set up properly and presented to participants in an appropriate way, they can be very effective for collecting diversity impact data. The following table shows a sample of the calculations from these questions for this particular diversity training program:

Partici pant	Annual Improvement Value	Basis for Value	Confid- ence	Isolation Factor	Adjusted Value
		Sample of Input from Participants in a Diversity Leadership and Mentoring Skills Program for New Managers			
11	$36,000	Improvement in efficiency of group. $3,000/ month x 12 (group estimate)	85%	50%	$15,300
42	$90,000	Turnover Reduction. Two turnover statistics per year. Base salary x 1.5 = $45,000	90%	40%	32,400
74	$24,000	Improvement in customer response time. (8hours to 6hours). Estimated value: $2,000/ month	60%	55%	$7,920
55	$2,000	5% in my effectiveness ($40,000 x 5%)	75%	50%	$750
96	$10,000	Absenteeism Reduction (50 absences per year x $200)	85%	75%	$6,375
117	$8,090	Team project completed 10 days ahead of schedule. Annual salaries $210,500 = $809 per day x 10 days	90%	45%	$3,276
118	$159,000	Under budget for the year by this amount	100%	30%	$47,700

Although this is an estimate, this approach does have considerable accuracy and credibility. Five adjustments are effectively utilized with this approach to reflect a conservative approach:

1. The individuals who do not respond to the questionnaire or provide usable data on the questionnaire are assumed to have no improvements. This is probably an overstatement since some individuals will have improvements, but not report them on the questionnaire.

2. Extreme data and incomplete, unrealistic, and unsupported claims are omitted from the analysis, although they may be included in the intangible benefits.

3. Since only annualized values are used, it is assumed that there are no benefits from the program after the first year of implementation. In reality, a diversity leadership and mentoring program should expect to add value perhaps for several years after training has been conducted and implemented.

4. The confidence level, expressed as a percent, is multiplied by the improvement value to reduce the amount of the improvement by the potential error.

5. The improvement amount is adjusted by the amount directly related to the diversity initiative, expressed as a percent.

When presented to senior management, the results of this diversity impact study were perceived to be an understatement of the diversity initiative's success. The data and the process were considered to be credible and accurate.

As an added enhancement to this method, management may be asked to review and approve the estimates from participants. In this way management can actually confirm the estimates, which enhances their credibility.

The process does have some disadvantages though. It is an estimate and, consequently, it does not have the accuracy desired by some managers. Also, the input data may be unreliable since some participants are incapable of providing these types of estimates. They may not be aware of exactly which factors contributed to the results.

Several advantages also make this strategy attractive. It is a simple process, easily understood by most diversity practitioners and others who review evaluation data. It is inexpensive, takes very little time and analysis, therefore it results in an efficient addition to the evaluation process. Estimates originate from a credible source—the individuals who actually produced the improvement.

The advantages seem to outweigh the disadvantages. Isolating the effects of diversity may never be totally precise. However, this estimate may be accurate enough for most clients and management groups. The process is appropriate when the participants are managers, supervisors, team leaders, sales associates, engineers, and other professional and technical employees.

Supervisor Estimates of Diversity's Impact

In lieu of, or in addition to, participant estimates, the participants' supervisor may be asked to provide the extent of diversity's role in producing a performance improvement. In some settings, participant's supervisors may be more familiar with the other factors influencing the change in performance. Consequently, they may be better equipped to provide estimates of impact.

Typical Questions to Ask Supervisors

- What percent of the improvement in performance measures of the participant resulted from the diversity initiative?
- What is the basis for this estimate?
- What is your confidence in this estimate, expressed as a percentage?
- What other factors could have contributed to this success?
- What other individuals or groups would know about this improvement and could estimate this percentage?
- Please list the factors with your estimates in the table provided.

The following table highlights an example of results that might be generated using the supervisor's input:

Sample of Results from Supervisor Estimates			
Location	Improvement	Percentage of improvement attributed to the diversity initiative	Dollar Value
A	To reduce low sales levels and customer attrition in targeted diverse customer market segments the multi-cultural marketing and language support initiative was installed. A five-percent increase in customer retention translated into a 125% increase in per customer profits.	50%	$3.2 Million
B	To reduce low sales levels and customer attrition in targeted diverse customer market segments the multi-cultural marketing and language support initiative was installed. A five-percent increase in customer retention translated into a 75% increase in per customer profits.	40%	1.4 Million
C	To reduce low sales levels and customer attrition in targeted diverse customer market segments the multi-cultural marketing and language support initiative was installed. A five-percent increase in customer retention translated into a 102% increase in per customer profits.	65%	$2.8 Million

The questions we asked in this section are essentially the same ones described in the participant's list of questions. Supervisor estimates should be analyzed in the same manner as participant estimates. To be more conservative, actual estimates may be adjusted by the confidence percentage. When participant's estimates have also been collected, the decision of which estimate to use becomes an issue. If there is some compelling reason to think that one estimate is more credible than the other is then it should be used. The most conservative approach is to use the lowest value and include appropriate explanations. Another potential option is to recognize that each source has its own unique perspective and that an average of the two is appropriate, placing an equal weight on each input. If it is possible, it is recommended that you obtain estimates from both the participant and the supervisor.

The advantages of this approach are similar to the advantages of participant estimation. It is simple and inexpensive and enjoys an acceptable degree of credibility because it comes directly from the supervisors of those individuals involved in the initiative. When combined with participant estimates, the credibility is enhanced considerably. Also, when factored by the level of confidence, its value further increases. The following example highlights a combined estimate.

Participant	Improvement (Dollar Value)	Basis	% Est. Partici.	% Est. Supv.	Conservative Integration	Average Value Integration
		Estimate of Diversity Impact from Participants and Supervisors **Food Service Laboratory Diversity Initiative**				
1	$5,500	Labor Savings	60%	50%	$2,750	$3,025
2	15,500	Turnover	50%	40%	6,000	6,750
3	9,300	Absenteeism	65%	75%	6,045	6,510
4	2,100	Shortages	90%	80%	1,680	1,785
5	0	--	--	--	--	--
6	29,000	Turnover	40%	50%	11,600	13,050
7	2,241	Inventory	70%	100%	1,569	1,905
8	3,621	Procedures	100%	90%	3,259	3,440
9	21,000	Turnover	75%	70%	14,700	15,225
10	1,500	Food Spoilage	100%	100%	1,500	1,500
11	15,000	Labor Savings	80%	70%	10,500	11,250
12	6,310	Accidents	70%	75%	4,417	4,575
13	14,500	Absenteeism	80%	75%	11,600	11,238
14	3,650	Productivity	100%	90%	3,285	3,468
Total	$128,722				$78,905	$83,721

Management Estimate of Diversity Impact

In some cases, upper management may estimate the percent of improvement that should be attributed to the diversity initiative's impact. Management may have additional information and a broader view of the factors influencing the improvement impact on the diversity initiative. If their deliberations about the value of the improvement are developed in a meeting of other top leaders, then the estimate has group ownership and extended credibility. While this process may be very subjective, the input is received from individuals who often provide or approve funding for diversity initiatives. Sometimes their level of comfort with the process is the most important consideration.

Considerations When Selecting Isolation Strategies

In this section, we only examined the use of three out of at least ten strategies for isolating diversity's contribution. Even with these, selecting the most appropriate strategies for the specific diversity initiative is difficult. Some strategies are simple and inexpensive, while others are more time consuming and costly. When attempting to make the selection decision, several factors should be considered:

- Feasibility of the strategy
- Accuracy provided with the strategy
- Credibility of the strategy with the target audience
- Specific costs to implement the strategy
- The amount of disruption in normal work activities as the strategy is implemented
- Participant, staff, and management time needed with the particular strategy

Multiple strategies or multiple sources for data input should be considered since two sources are usually better than one. When multiple sources are utilized, a conservative method is recommended to combine the inputs. A conservative approach builds acceptance. The target audience should always be provided with explanations of the process and the various subjective factors involved.

Multiple sources allow an organization to experiment with different strategies and build confidence with a particular strategy. For example, if management is concerned about the accuracy of the participant's estimates, a combination of control group arrangement and participant's estimates could be attempted to check the accuracy of the estimation process.

**What to Do
Next**

Application Exercise

1. Using a previous diversity initiative you have implemented, identify other possible contributing factors that were not identified.

   _____

   _____

2. Given the considerations when selecting diversity isolation strategies, identify the strategy you would have used in this initiative and your reason(s) for selecting it.

   _____

   _____

   _____

How to Calculate Diversity ROI

Many DROI Initiative Will Generate Large Returns

It is not unusual for the ROI in diversity initiatives to be extremely large. Even when portion of the improvement is allocated to other factors, the numbers are still impressive in many situations. The audience should understand that, although every effort was made to isolate the diversity impact, it is still a figure that is not precise and may contain a certain amount of error…similar to some other estimated business calculations such as inflation, actuarial table estimates, etc. It represents the best estimate of the impact given the constraints, conditions, and resources available. Chances are the diversity isolation strategies are more accurate than other types of analysis regularly utilized in other functions within the organization.

Too often results are reported and linked to diversity without any attempt to isolate the portion of the results that can be attributed to diversity. If the diversity practice is to continue to improve its professional image as well as to meet its responsibility for obtaining results, this issue must be addressed early in the process.

Step 4 – Convert the Contribution to Money

Step 4 – Convert the Contribution to Money

Introduction

In many evaluation impact studies, the examination usually stops with the tabulation of business results. In those situations, the initiative is considered successful if it produced improvements such as turnover reduction, improved customer satisfaction, reduced absenteeism or the like. While these results are important, it is more insightful to compare the value of the results to the cost of the initiative. This allows the initiative to be primed to calculate its return on investment.

Identifying the Hard and Soft Data Contained in the Diversity Contribution

After collecting diversity performance data, it is helpful to divide the data into hard and soft categories. Hard data are the traditional measures of organizational performance. They are objective, easy to measure, and easy to convert to monetary values. Hard data are often very common measures, they achieve high credibility with management, and are available in every type of organization.

How to Calculate Diversity ROI

Hard data represent the output, quality, cost, and time of work-related processes. The table below shows a sampling of typical hard data under these four categories.

Examples of Hard Data	
Output	**Time**
▪ Units Produced	▪ Equipment Downtime
▪ Tons Manufactured	▪ Overtime
▪ Forms Processed	▪ On-time Shipments
▪ Items Sold	▪ Processing Time
▪ Inventory Turnover	▪ Supervisor Time
▪ Patients Visited	▪ Training Time
▪ Productivity	▪ Efficiency
▪ New Accounts Opened	▪ Work Stoppages
▪ Students Graduated	▪ Lost Time Days
Costs	**Quality**
▪ Budget Variances	▪ Scrap
▪ Unit Costs	▪ Waste
▪ Costs by Account	▪ Rejects
▪ Number of Cost Reductions	▪ Product Defects
▪ Accident Costs	▪ Number of Accidents
▪ Sales Expense	▪ Rework
▪ Program Costs	▪ Percent of Tasks Completed Properly
▪ Fixed Costs	
▪ Variable Costs	▪ Product Failures

Almost every department or unit will have hard data performance measures. For example, a cross-functional team in a government office approving applications for work visas will have these four measures among its overall performance measurement: the number of applications processed (Output), cost per applications processed (Cost), the number of errors made in processing applications (Quality), and the time it takes to process and approve an application (Time). Ideally, diversity initiatives in this example can be linked to one or more hard data measures.

Because many diversity initiatives are more heavily related to soft skills, soft data are often reviewed in diversity measurement studies. Soft data are usually subjective, behaviorally oriented, sometimes difficult to measure, and almost always difficult to convert to monetary values. When compared to hard data, soft data are usually seen as less credible as a performance measure.

Soft data items can be grouped into several categories as shown in the following table.

Examples of Soft Data	
Work Habits	**New Skills**
▪ Absenteeism ▪ Tardiness ▪ Violations of Safety Rules ▪ Number of Communications Breakdowns ▪ Follow-up	▪ Decisions Made ▪ Problems Solved ▪ Conflicts Avoided ▪ Grievances Resolved ▪ Counseling Success ▪ Intention to Use New Skills ▪ Frequency of Use of New Skills
Work Climate	**Development/Advancement**
▪ Number of Grievances ▪ Number of Discrimination Charges ▪ Employee Complaints ▪ Job Satisfaction ▪ Employee Turnover ▪ Litigation ▪ Work Life Satisfaction ▪ Career Advancement Satisfaction	▪ Number of Promotions ▪ Number of Pay Increases ▪ Number of Diversity Training Programs Attended ▪ Requests for Transfer ▪ Performance Appraisal Ratings ▪ Increases in Job Effectiveness
Attitude	**Initiative**
▪ Favorable Reactions ▪ Attitude Changes ▪ Perceptions of Job Responsibilities ▪ Perceived Changes in Performance ▪ Employee Loyalty ▪ Increased Confidence	▪ Implementation of New Ideas ▪ Successful Completion of Projects ▪ Number of Suggestions Implemented ▪ Setting Goals and Objectives

Measures such as employee turnover, absenteeism, and grievances appear as soft data items, not because they are difficult to measure, but because it is difficult to accurately convert them to monetary values.

Basic Steps to Convert Data

Before describing some specific strategies to convert either hard or soft data to monetary values, the basic steps used to convert data in each strategy are highlighted here. These steps should be followed for each data conversion process.

Focus on the Unit of Measure. First, identify a unit of improvement. For output data, the unit of measure is the item produced, service provided or sale consummated. Time measures are varied and include items such as the time to complete a project, cycle time, or customer response time. The unit is usually expressed as minutes, hours, or days. Quality is a common measure, and the unit may be one error, reject, defect, or rework item. Soft data measures are varied, and the unit of improvement may include items such as a grievance, an absence, an employee turnover statistic, or a one-point change in the customer satisfaction index.

Determine the Value of Each Unit. Place a value (V) on the unit identified in the first step. For measures of production, quality, cost, and time, the process is relatively easy. Most organizations have records or reports reflecting the value of items such as one unit of production or the cost of a defect. Soft data are more difficult to convert to a value, since the cost of one absence, one grievance, or a one-point change in the diversity attitude survey is often difficult to pinpoint. The array of strategies offered in this chapter will include a variety of techniques to make this conversion. When more than one value is available, either the most credible or the lowest value should be used.

Calculate the Change in Performance Data. Calculate the change in output data after the effects of the diversity initiative have been isolated from other influences. The change (ΔP) is the performance improvement, measured as hard or soft data, that is directly attributable to the diversity initiative. The value may represent the performance improvement for individuals, a team, a group or several groups of participants or an organization.

Determine an Annual Amount for the Change. Annualize the ΔP value to develop a total change in the performance data for one year. This procedure has become a standard approach with many organizations that wish to capture the total benefits of the diversity initiative. Although the benefits may not be realized at the same level for an entire year, some diversity initiatives will continue to produce benefits beyond one year. Therefore, using one year of benefits is considered a conservative approach.

Calculate the Total Value of the Improvement. Develop the total value of improvement by multiplying the annual performance change (ΔP) by the unit value (V) for the complete performance group in question. For example, if one group of participants for a diversity initiative is being evaluated, the total value will include the total improvement for all participants in the group. This value for annual diversity initiative benefits is then compared to the cost of the diversity initiative usually through the diversity return on investment (DROI) calculation.

Strategies for Converting Data to Monetary Values

An example taken from a cross-functional team building initiative at a manufacturing plant describes the five-step process of converting data to monetary values. This initiative was developed and implemented after a needs assessment revealed that a lack of teamwork was causing an excessive number of grievances. This diversity initiative was designed to reduce the number of grievances filed at Step two. This is the step in which the grievance is recorded in writing and becomes a measurable soft data item. Therefore, the actual number of grievances resolved at Step two in the grievance process was selected as an output measure. The table

How to Calculate Diversity ROI

diagram below illustrates the steps taken to assign a monetary value to the data. The total monetary impact of this diversity initiative was $546,000.

	An Example of the Steps to Convert Data to Monetary Values
	Setting: Cross-functional Teambuilding Initiative in a Manufacturing Plant
Steps	**Description**
1	*Focus on a Unit of Improvement* One grievance reaching Step two in the four-step grievance resolution process
2	*Determine a Value of Each Unit* Using internal experts—the labor relations staff and the diversity staff—the cost of an average grievance was estimated to be $6,500 when considering time and direct costs. (V = $6,500)
3	*Calculate the Change in Performance Data* Six months after the initiative was completed, total grievances per month reaching Step two declined by ten. Seven of the ten grievance reductions were related to the diversity initiative as determined by supervisors (*Isolating the Effects of Diversity*)
4	*Determine an Annual Amount for the Change* Using the six month value, seven per month, yields an annual improvement of 84 (ΔP)
5	*Calculate the Annual Value of the Improvement* Annual Value = ΔP x V $\qquad$ = 84 x $6,500 $\qquad$ = $546,000

There are a number of strategies available to convert data to monetary values. Some of the strategies are appropriate for a specific type of data category, while other strategies can be used with virtually any type of data. We will explore a few of these strategies in detail in this section of the book. Additional strategies are taught in the "Calculating Diversity Return on Investment Workshop" mentioned earlier. In general, the Diversity staff's challenge is to select the particular strategy that best matches the type of data and situation. Several strategies are presented in the next section, beginning with the most credible approach.

Strategy: Converting Output Data to Contribution

When a diversity initiative has produced a change in output, the value of the increased output can usually be determined from the organization's accounting or operating records. For organizations operating on a profit basis, this value is usually the marginal profit contribution of an additional unit of production, unit of sale, or unit of service provided. For example, a diverse, cross-functional sales team in a major appliance manufacturer is able to boost sales of small refrigerators in multi-ethnic markets with a series of comprehensive multicultural marketing and sales training programs. The unit of improvement, therefore, is the profit margin of one refrigerator.

In organizations that are performance rather than profit driven, this value is usually reflected in the savings accumulated when an additional unit of output is realized for the same input requirements. For example, in the visa section of a government office, an additional visa application is processed at no additional cost. Therefore, an increase in output translates into a cost savings equal to the unit cost of processing a visa.

The formulas and calculations used to measure this contribution depend on the organization and its records. Most organizations have this type of data readily available for performance monitoring and goal setting. Managers often use marginal cost statements and sensitivity analyses to pinpoint the value associated with changes in output. If the data are not available, the diversity staff must initiate or coordinate the development of the appropriate values.

An example involving a commercial bank shows that a multi-ethnic market sales seminar for consumer loan officers was conducted that resulted in additional consumer loan volume in new, multi-ethnic markets (output). To measure the return on investment in this diversity initiative, it is necessary to calculate the value (profit contribution) of one additional consumer loan. This is a relatively easy item to calculate from bank records. The following table shows several components that are necessary for this calculation.

Loan Profitability Analysis	
Profit Contribution	**Unit Value**
Average Loan Size	$15,500
Average Loan Yield	9.75%
Average Cost of Funds (including branch costs)	5.50%
Direct Costs for Consumer Lending	0.82%
Corporate Overhead	1.61%
Net Profit Per Loan	**1.82%**

The first step is to determine the yield, which is available from bank records. Next, the average spread between the cost of funds and the yield received on the loan is calculated. For example, the bank could obtain funds from depositors at 5.5% on average, including the cost of operating the branches. The direct costs of making the loan, such as salaries of employees directly involved in consumer lending and advertising costs in current and new ethnic markets for consumer loans, has to be subtracted from the difference. When conducting a historical analysis of costs, these direct costs amounted to 0.82% of the loan value. To cover overhead costs for other corporate functions, an additional 1.61% was subtracted from the value. The remaining 1.82% of the average loan value represented the bank's profit margin on a loan. These are just a few examples to demonstrate methods used in converting output data to contribution strategy. Let's examine another strategy.

Strategy: Calculating the Cost of Quality

Quality is a critical issue, and its costs are an important issue in most manufacturing and service firms. Since some diversity initiatives can be designed to improve quality, the diversity staff must increase its understanding of and place a high value on improving certain quality measures. For some quality measures, the task is easy. For example, if quality is measured with a defect rate, the value of the improvement is the cost to repair or replace the product. The most obvious cost of poor quality is the scrap or waste generated by mistakes, poor communication, or conflicts in work style. Defective products, spoiled raw materials, and discarded paperwork are all results of poor quality. This scrap and waste translates directly into monetary value. For example, in a production environment, the costs of a defective product is the total cost incurred up to the point the mistake is identified minus the salvage value.

Employee mistakes and errors can cause expensive rework. The most costly rework occurs when a product is delivered to a customer and must be returned for correction. The cost of rework includes both labor and direct costs. In some organizations, the cost of rework can be as much as 35% of operating costs. Perhaps the costliest element of poor quality is customer and client dissatisfaction. In some cases, serious mistakes can result in lost business. Customer dissatisfaction is difficult to quantify, and attempts to arrive at a monetary value may be impossible using direct methods. Usually the judgment and expertise of sales, marketing, or quality managers or someone who is familiar with the customer market's behavior when dissatisfaction occurs are the best sources by which to try to measure the impact of dissatisfaction. A growing number of quality experts are measuring customer and client dissatisfaction with market surveys. However, other strategies discussed in this chapter may be more appropriate to measure the cost of customer dissatisfaction.

Strategy: Converting Employee Time

Reduction in employee time is a common objective for diversity's impact on organizational performance. In a team environment, a diversity initiative focused on diverse and cross-functional teamwork skills development could enable a team to perform a task in a shorter time frame, or with fewer people. The most obvious time savings are from labor reduction costs in performing work. The monetary savings is found by multiplying the hours saved times the labor cost per hour. For example, if after attending a diverse work group teambuilding workshop, participants estimate they each save an average of 74 minutes per day, worth $31.25 per day or $7,500 per year (240 work days times $31.25), then this is an added value to the organization. This timesaving is based on the average salary plus benefits for the typical participant. If the program has 25 participants, then the total annual savings is $187,500.

The average wage with a percent added for employee benefits will suffice for most calculations. However, employee time may be worth more. For example, additional costs in maintaining an employee (office space, furniture, telephone, utilities, computers, secretarial support, an other overhead expenses) could be included in the average labor cost. Therefore, the average wage rate may quickly grow to a large number. However, the conservative approach is to use the salary plus employee benefits method.

In addition to the labor cost per hour, other benefits can result from a timesaving. These include improved service, avoidance of penalties for late projects, and the creation of additional opportunities for profit. These values can be estimated using other methods.

A word of caution is in order when timesavings are developed. Timesaving is only realized when the amount of time saved translates into a cost reduction or profit contribution. If a diversity initiative results in a savings in manager time, a monetary value is realized only if the manager used the additional time in a productive way. If a diverse, cross-functional team-based program generates a new process that eliminates several hours of work each day, the actual savings will be realized only if there is a cost savings from a reduction in employees or a reduction in overtime pay. Therefore, an important preliminary step in developing timesavings is to determine if a "true" saving will be realized.

Strategy: Using Historical Costs

Sometimes historical records contain the value of a measure and reflect the cost (or value) of a unit of improvement. This strategy involves identifying the appropriate records and tabulating the actual cost components for the item in question. For example, a large construction firm implemented an initiative to improve safety performance. The program improved several safety-related performance measures ranging from OSHA fines to total worker compensation costs. Examining the company's records using one year of data, the diversity and HR staff calculated the average cost for each safety measure.

Historical data are usually available for most hard data. Unfortunately, this is generally not true for soft data, and thus, other strategies must be employed to convert the data to monetary values.

Strategy: Using Internal and External Experts' Input

When faced with converting soft data items for which historical records are not available, it might be feasible to consider input from experts on the processes. With this approach, internal experts provide the cost (or value) of one unit of improvement. Those individuals who have knowledge of the situation and the respect of the management group are often the best prospects for expert input. These experts must understand the processes and be willing to provide estimates as well as the assumptions used in arriving at the estimate. When requesting input from these individuals, it is best to explain the full scope of what is needed, providing as many specifics as possible. Most experts have their own methodology to develop this value.

Using the earlier example of the teambuilding initiative that was designed to reduce the number of grievances filed at Step two, we can illustrate how an expert's help may be necessary. Remember, Step two is the step in which the grievance is recorded in writing and becomes a measurable soft data item. Except for actual cost settlements and direct external costs, what if the organization had no records of the total costs of grievances (i.e., there is no data for the time required to resolve a grievance). In this case, an estimate would be needed from an expert. The manager of labor relations, who had credibility with senior management and thorough knowledge of the grievance process, provided an estimate of the cost. She based her cost estimate on the average settlement when a grievance was lost, the direct cost related to the grievances (arbitration, legal fees, printing, research), the estimated amount of the supervisory, staff, and employee time associated with the grievance, and a factor for reduced morale. The internal estimate, although not a precise figure, was appropriate for this analysis and had adequate credibility with management.

When internal experts are not available, external experts are recruited. External experts must be selected based on their experience with the unit of measure. Fortunately, many experts are available who work directly with important measures such as employee attitudes, customer satisfaction, turnover, absenteeism, grievances, new markets and the like. They are often willing to provide estimates of the cost (or value) of these items. Because the credibility of the value is directly related to his or her reputation, the credibility and reputation of the expert are critical.

This need to periodically use internal and external experts highlights the advantages of a diverse, cross-functional team working together on a diversity return on investment study.

How to Calculate Diversity ROI

Selecting the Appropriate Strategy

There are many strategies available to convert the contribution to money. The real challenge is selecting the most appropriate strategy to meet the needs of the situation. The following guidelines can help determine the proper selection.

Use the Strategy Appropriate for the Type of Data. Some strategies are designed specifically for hard data, while others are more appropriate for soft data. Consequently, the actual type of data will often dictate the strategy. Hard data, while always preferred, are not always available. Soft data are often required and therefore must be addressed with the appropriate strategy.

Move from the Most Accurate to the Least Accurate Strategies. The selected strategies presented in this section are presented in the order of accuracy and credibility, beginning with the most credible. Working down the list, each strategy should be considered for its feasibility in the situation. The strategy with the most accuracy is recommended, if it is feasible.

Consider Availability and Convenience When Selecting Strategies. Sometimes the availability of a particular source of data will drive the selection. In other situations, the convenience of a technique may be an important factor in selecting the strategy.

When Estimates are Sought, Use the Source Who has the Broadest Perspective on the Issue. The person providing an estimate must be knowledgeable on the processes and the issues surrounding the value of the data.

Use Multiple Strategies When Feasible. Sometimes it is helpful to have more than one strategy for obtaining a value for the data. When multiple sources are available, more than one source should be used to serve as a comparison or provide another perspective. When multiple sources are used, the data must be integrated using a convenient decision rule such as the lowest value. This is preferred because of the conservative nature of the lowest value.

Minimize the Amount of Time Required to Select and Implement the Appropriate Strategy. As with other processes, it is important to keep the time invested as low as possible, so that the total time and effort for the diversity ROI study does not become excessive. Some strategies can be implemented with less time than others. Too much time at this step can dampen an otherwise enthusiastic attitude about the process. Remember, diversity is often held to a double standard and excessive scrutiny which can cause diversity practitioners to be overly cautious about this process.

Accuracy and Credibility of the Data

The Credibility Problem

The strategies presented in this chapter assume that each data item collected and linked with training can be converted to a monetary value. Although estimates can be developed using one or more strategies, the process of converting data to monetary values may lose credibility with the target audience, who may doubt its use in analysis. Very subjective data, such as change in employee morale or a reduction in the number of employee conflicts, are difficult to convert to monetary values. The key question for this determination is this: "Could these results be presented to senior management with confidence?" If the process does not meet this credibility test, the data should not be converted to monetary values and instead listed as an intangible benefit. Other data, particularly hard data items, could be used in the diversity ROI calculation, leaving the very subjective data as intangible improvements.

The accuracy of data and the credibility of the conversion process are important concerns. Diversity professionals sometimes avoid converting data because of these issues.

They are more comfortable in reporting that a diversity initiative resulted in reducing absenteeism from 6% to 4% without attempting to place a value on the improvement. They assume that each person receiving the information will place a value on the absenteeism reduction. Unfortunately, the target audience may know little about the cost of absenteeism and will usually underestimate the actual value of the improvement. Consequently, there should be some attempt to include this conversion in the diversity return on investment calculation.

How the Credibility of Data is Influenced

When diversity ROI data are presented to selected target audiences, data credibility may be an issue. The degree to which the target audience will believe the data will be influenced by the following factors:

Influence Factors

Reputation of the source data	The actual source of the data represents the first credibility issue. How credible is the individual or groups providing the data? Do they understand the issues? Are they knowledgeable of all of the processes? The target audience will often place more credibility on the data obtained from those

	Influence Factors
	who are closest to the source of the actual improvement or change.
Reputation of the source of the study	The target audience scrutinizes the reputation of the individual, group, or organization presenting the data. Do they have a history of providing accurate reports? Are they unbiased with their analyses? Are they fair in their presentation? Answers to these and other questions will form an impression about the reputation.
Motives of the evaluators	Do the individuals presenting the data have an ax to grind? Do they have a personal interest in creating a favorable or unfavorable result? These issues will cause the target audience to examine the motive of those who have conducted the study.
Methodology of the study	The audience will want to know specifically how the research was conducted, how the calculations were made, what steps were followed, what processes were used, etc. A lack of information on the methodology will cause the audience to become suspicious of

Influence Factors	
	the results.
Assumptions made in the analysis	In many diversity return on investment studies, assumptions are made on which the calculations and conclusions are based. What are the assumptions? Are they standard? How do they compare with other assumptions in other studies? When assumptions are omitted, the audience will substitute their own, often unfavorable assumptions.
Realism of the outcome data	Impressive diversity ROI values could cause problems. When outcomes appear to be unrealistic, it may be difficult for the target audience to believe them. Huge claims often fall on deaf ears, causing reports to be thrown away before they are reviewed in detail.
Type of data	The target audience will usually have a preference for hard data. They are seeking business performance data tied to output, quality, costs, and time. These measures are usually easily understood and relate closely to organizational performance. On the other hand, soft data may be reviewed suspiciously

Influence Factors	
	from the outset. Many senior managers are concerned about the soft nature and limitations of the data included in the analysis.
Scope of analysis	Is the scope of the analysis very narrow? Does it involve just one group or all of the employees in the organization? Limiting the diversity ROI study to a small group or a series of groups of employees makes the process more accurate.

Collectively, these factors will influence the credibility of the diversity ROI study and provide a framework from which to develop your diversity ROI study report. Therefore, when you are considering each of the issues, the following key points are suggested:

- Use the most credible and reliable sources for your estimates
- Present the material in an unbiased way
- Fully explain the methodology used throughout the process, preferably in a step-by-step manner.
- Define the assumptions made in the analysis, and compare them to assumptions made in similar studies.
- Consider factoring or adjusting output values when they appear to be unrealistic to a conservative level

- Use hard data whenever possible and combine with soft data if available.

- Keep the scope of the analysis very narrow. Conduct the impact with one or more groups or participants.

Making Adjustments

Two potential adjustments should be considered before finalizing the monetary value. In some organizations where soft data are used and values are derived with imprecise methods, senior executives are sometimes offered the opportunity to review and approve the data. Because of the subjective nature of this process, management may factor (reduce) the data such that the final results are more credible.

The other adjustment concerns the time value of money. Since an investment in a diversity initiative is made at one time period and the return is realized in a later time period, a few organizations adjust the program benefits to reflect the time value of money, using discounted cash flow techniques. The actual monetary benefits of the program are adjusted for this time period. The amount of this adjustment, however, is usually small compared with the typical benefits realized from diversity initiatives and interventions.

How to Calculate Diversity ROI

Application Exercise

Using the diversity initiative you identified in *Step 3* (in the previous chapter), use the "Basic steps to convert data" , shown in this chapter, to convert your initiative data to a monetary value:

What to Do Next

➢ *Unit of Improvement:* _____

➢ *Value of each unit:* _____

➢ *Change in performance data:* _____

➢ *Determine annual amount:* _____

➢ *Calculate annual value of Improvement:* _____

As diversity professionals, we must go beyond simply reporting general reactions to diversity initiatives as evidence of diversity progress. We must take the additional steps to complete the following tasks:

➢ Integrate diversity into business operations
➢ Track and measure diversity results in quantitative and qualitative terms
➢ Report changes in business performance
➢ And convert business results data to monetary values and compare them to program costs as a means to compute benefit-to-cost ratios and diversity return on investment percentages

When this is done, diversity will be set on par with other strategic business initiatives.

Step 5 – Calculate the Costs, Benefits and DROI

Step 5 – Calculate the Costs, Benefits and DROI

Introduction

Taking the time to calculate the costs and benefits of a diversity initiative is an essential step in developing the Diversity Return on Investment calculation since it represents the denominator in the DROI formula. It is equally critical to pay attention to both the costs and benefits of any diversity initiative that you put in place. In practice, however, the costs are often more easily captured than benefits. This chapter of the book highlights some specific methods for accumulating and calculating costs, outlining the specific costs that should be captured, identifying benefits as well as identifying the steps to perform a DROI calculation.

Strategies for Accumulating and Calculating Costs

Importance of Costs

Capturing costs is challenging because the figures must be accurate, reliable and realistic. Although most organizations develop costs with a lot less difficulty than developing the economic value of the benefits, calculating the true cost and benefits of diversity can be difficult. And of course, this affects the Diversity Return on Investment. On the cost side, the total diversity organization budget is usually a number that is easily developed, however, determining the specific costs of a diversity initiative, including related indirect costs, and its benefits can be far more elusive. To develop a realistic DROI, costs must be accurate and credible. Otherwise, the painstaking difficulty and attention to benefits will be wasted because of inadequate or inaccurate costs.

Today there is more pressure than ever before to report all initiative costs or what is commonly referred to as fully loaded costs. This takes the cost profile beyond the direct cost of diversity initiatives and includes the time all participants are involved in developing and participating in the initiative, including all costs, benefits, and other overhead. Taking the conservative approach to calculate diversity return on investment, you should plan to report fully loaded costs. With this approach, all costs that can be identified and linked to a particular diversity initiative are included. The philosophy is simple: When in doubt in the denominator, put it in (i.e., if it is questionable whether a cost should be included, the rule suggests that it should be included, even if the organizational costs guidelines don't require it). When diversity ROI is reported to your target audiences, it should withstand even the closest scrutiny in terms of its accuracy and credibility.

The only way to meet this test is to ensure that all costs are included.

The Impact of Reporting Costs Without Benefits

It is dangerous to communicate the costs of diversity initiatives without presenting the corresponding benefits. Unfortunately, many organizations have fallen into this trap. Because costs can be easily collected, they are presented to management in all types of ingenious ways such as cost of the initiative, cost per diversity hire, and cost per diversity training hour and the like. While these may be helpful for efficiency comparisons, it may present a real problem if they are presented without the benefit side of the story. When executives review diversity initiative costs, a logical question comes to mind: What benefit was received for this investment in diversity? This can be a typical management reaction, particularly when costs are perceived to be very high. Some organizations have adopted a policy of not communicating diversity initiatives costs data unless the benefits can be captured and presented along with the costs. Even if the benefit data are subjective and intangible, they are included with the cost data. This helps keep balance when diversity efforts are viewed by others.

How to Calculate Diversity ROI

Typical Cost Categories

One of the most important tasks you must complete is to define which specific costs are included in the tabulation of costs in a diversity initiative. This task involves decisions that will be made by the diversity staff and usually approved by management. If appropriate, the finance and accounting staff may need to approve the list. The following table shows the recommended cost categories for a fully loaded, conservative approach to estimating costs. Each category is described in the paragraphs that follow.

Calculate the Costs, Benefits and DROI

Diversity Initiative Cost Categories		
Cost Item	**Prorated**	**Expensed**
Needs Assessment	✓	
Design and Development	✓	
Acquisition	✓	
Delivery Internal		✓
▪ Salaries/Benefits-Facilitators/Diversity Council Members		✓
▪ Materials and Fees		✓
▪ Travel/Lodging/Meals		✓
▪ Facilities		✓
▪ Salaries/Benefits-Participants		✓
▪ Contact Time		✓
▪ Travel Time		✓
▪ Preparation Time		✓
Evaluation	✓	
Overhead/Diversity Department	✓	

Prorated vs. Direct Costs

Usually all costs related to a diversity initiative or project are captured and expensed to that initiative or project. However, three categories are usually prorated over several sessions of the same project or initiative. Needs assessment, design and development, and acquisition are all significant costs that should be prorated over a basic shelf life of the diversity initiative. With a conservative approach, the shelf life of a diversity initiative should be very short. Some organizations consider one year of operation, others may consider two or three years. If there is some question about the specific time period to be used in the proration formula, the finance and accounting staff should be consulted.

A brief example will illustrate the proration for development costs. In a large industrial organization, a diversity initiative was created to improve multicultural teamwork and innovation at a cost of $98,000. The diversity initiative's development team anticipated that the project would have a three-year life cycle before it would have to be updated. The revision costs at the end of the three years were estimated to be about one-half of the original development costs, or $49,000. The diversity project would be conducted with 25 groups in a three-year period, with a DROI calculation planned for one specific group. Since the project would have one-half of its residual value at the end of three years, one-half of the cost should be written off for this three-year period. Thus, the $49,000, representing half of the development costs, would be spread over the 25 groups as a prorated development cost. Therefore, a DROI for one group would have a development cost of approximately $2,000 ($49,000/25 = $1,960) included in the cost profile.

Benefits Factor

When presenting participant and diversity staff salaries associated with diversity initiatives, the benefits factor should be included. This number is usually well known in the organization and is used in other costing formulas. It represents the cost of all employee benefits expressed as a percent of base salaries. In some organizations, this value is as high as 50%-60%. In others, it may be as low as 25%-30%. The average in the USA is 38% (Annual Employee Benefits Report, Nations Business, January 1996,p28).

Needs Assessment

One of the most often overlooked items is the cost of conducting a needs assessment in the exploratory phase of a diversity audit. In some diversity initiatives, this cost is zero because the diversity initiative is conducted without a needs assessment (such as mandatory diversity awareness training in some organizations). However, as more organizations focus increased attention on identifying a validated need for an initiative or project, this item will become a more significant cost in the future. All costs associated with the needs assessment should be captured to the fullest extent possible. These costs include the time of staff members conducting the assessment, direct fees and expenses for external consultants who conduct the needs assessment, and internal services and supplies used in the analysis. The total costs are usually prorated over the life of the diversity initiative or project. Depending on the type and nature of the diversity initiative, the shelf life should be kept to a very reasonable number in the one- to two-year timeframe. Of course the exception would be very expensive initiatives (such as building a daycare facility and its operation) which are not expected to change significantly for several years.

Design and Development Costs

One of the more significant items is the cost of designing and developing the initiative. These costs include internal staff time in both design and development and the purchase of supplies, equipment, materials, audio-visual media, and other items directly related to the diversity initiative. It would also include the use of consultants. As with the needs assessment costs, design and development costs are usually prorated, perhaps using the same timeframe. One or two years is recommended unless the initiative is not expected to change for many years and the costs are very significant.

Acquisition Costs

In lieu of development costs, many organizations will purchase some diversity programs to use directly or in a modified format. This is often the case with diversity training materials. The acquisition costs for these programs include the purchase price for the instructional materials, train-the-trainer sessions, licensing agreements, and other costs associated with the right to deliver the program. These acquisition costs should be prorated using the same rationale outlined for design and development costs; one to two years should be sufficient. If modification of the program is needed or some additional development is required, these costs should be included as development costs. In practice, many diversity-training programs have both acquisition costs and development costs.

Delivery Costs

Usually the largest segment of the diversity initiative costs would be those associated with delivering the initiative. Five major categories are included.

Salaries of Facilitators/Diversity Council Members. The salaries of facilitators or diversity council members should be included. If a facilitator or council member is involved in more than one program, the time should be allocated to the specific program under review. If external facilitators are used, all charges should be included for the session. The important issue is to capture all of the direct time of internal employees or external consultants who work directly with the diversity initiative. The benefits factor should be included each time direct labor cost are involved. This factor is a widely accepted value, usually generated by the finance and accounting staff. It is usually in the range of 30%-40%.

How to Calculate Diversity ROI

Diversity Project Materials and Fees. Specific diversity initiative materials such as notebooks, textbooks, case studies, exercises, speakers on key topics, and participant workbooks should be included in the delivery costs, along with license fees, user fees, and royalty payments. Pens, paper, certificates, and calculators are also included in this category.

Travel, Lodging, and Meals. Direct travel for participants, facilitators, diversity council members, or others is included. Lodging and meals are included for participants during travel, as well as meals during the stay if they are participating in education or training-based diversity initiatives. Refreshments should also be included.

Facilities. The direct cost of any purchased facilities should be included. For external programs, this is the direct charge from conference centers, hotels, or motels. If the diversity initiative is implemented and an in-house facility is used that represents a cost to the organization, the cost should be estimated and included, even if it is not the practice to include facilities' costs in other reports.

Participant' Salaries and Benefits. The salaries plus employee benefits of participants represent an expense that should be included. For situations where the diversity initiative has already taken place, these costs can be estimated using average or midpoint values for salaries in typical job classifications. When a program is targeted for a DROI calculation, participants can provide their actual salaries directly and in a confidential manner.

Evaluation

Usually the total evaluation costs is included in the diversity initiative's costs to compute the fully loaded cost. DROI costs include the cost of developing the evaluation strategy, designing instruments, collecting data, data analysis, and report preparation and distribution. Cost categories include time, materials, purchased instruments, or surveys. A case can be made to prorate the evaluation costs over several programs instead of charging the total amount as an expense. For example, if 25 sessions of a training-based diversity initiative are conducted in a three-year period and one group is selected for a DROI study, then the DROI costs could logically be prorated over the 25 sessions. Since the results of the DROI analysis should reflect the success of the other programs as will perhaps result in changes that will influence the other programs as well.

Overhead

A final charge is the cost of overhead, the additional costs in the diversity function not directly related to a particular diversity initiative. The overhead category represents and diversity department cost not considered in the above calculations. Typical items include the cost of clerical support, the departmental office expenses, salaries of the diversity department staff members (this is prorated if diversity is not your full-time job responsibility, e.g., you have other functions attached to your job such as EEO, Organizational Effectiveness, etc.), and other fixed costs. Some organizations obtain an estimate for allocation by dividing the total overhead by the number of diversity initiative days for the year (examining how many days you spent or will spend involved in an actual diversity initiative for the year). This becomes a standard value to use in calculations.

Costs are important and should be fully loaded in the DROI calculation. From a practical standpoint, including some of the costs may be optional, based upon the organization's guidelines and philosophy. However, because of the scrutiny involved in DROI calculations, it is recommended that all costs are included, even if it goes beyond the requirements of the company policy.

Defining Return on Investment

The term "return on Investment (ROI) in diversity is often misunderstood and misused. In some situations, a very broad definition for ROI includes any benefit from the program. In these situations, ROI is a vague concept in which even subjective data linked to the diversity effort is included in the concept of the return. The expression originates in finance and accounting and usually refers to the pre-tax contribution measured against controllable assets. In formula form it is expressed as:

Average ROI = $\underline{\text{pretax earnings}}$

average investment

It measures the anticipated profitability of an investment and is used as a standard measure of the performance of divisions or profit centers within a business.

The investment portion of the formula represents capital expenditures such as a training facility for the diversity awareness program or equipment plus initial development or production costs. The original investment figure or production costs can be used. Also, the original investment figure can be used, or the present book value can be expressed as the average investment over a period of time. If the diversity program is a one-time offering, then the figure is the original investment.

However, if the initial costs are spread over a period of time, then the average book value is usually more appropriate. This value is essentially half the initial costs since, through depreciation, a certain fixed part of investment is written off each year over the life of the investment.

How to Calculate Diversity ROI

In many situations, a group of employees are to be trained in diversity at one time, so the investment figure is the total cost of analysis, development, delivery, and evaluation lumped together for the bottom part of the equation. The benefits are then calculated assuming that all participants attend the program or have attended the program, depending on whether the return is a prediction or a reflection of what has happened.

To keep calculations simple, it is recommended that the return be based on pretax conditions. This avoids the issue of investment tax credits, depreciation, tax shields, and other related items.

Sound complicated? It can be, depending on the particular accounting methodology you subscribe to. For the purposes of calculating diversity's return on investment in the "live laboratory of organizations, we will use an effective, simple, straightforward accounting approach.

In this book, Diversity Return on Investment (DROI) is more precise and is meant to represent an actual value developed by comparing the diversity initiative costs to benefits. The two most common measures are the cost/benefit ratio and the (DROI) formula. Both are presented here along with other approaches that calculate a return.

Calculate the Costs, Benefits and DROI

For some time now, diversity practitioners and researchers have tried to calculate the actual return on investment in diversity. If diversity is considered an investment—not an expense—then it is appropriate to place the diversity investment in the same funding process as other investments, such as the investment in equipment and facilities. Although these other investments are quite different, management often views them in the same way. Thus, it is critical to the success of the diversity field to develop specific values that reflect Diversity's Return on Investment (DROI).

To illustrate this calculation, assume that a work-life and family training program had initial costs of $50,000. The program will have a useful life of three years with negligible residual value at that time. During the three-year period, the program produces a net savings of $30,000, or $10,000 per year ($30,000/3). The average investment is $25,000 ($50,000/2) since the average book value is essentially half the costs. The average return is:

Average ROI = $\dfrac{\text{annual savings}}{\text{average investment}}$

$\qquad\quad = \dfrac{\$10,000}{\$25,000}$

$\qquad\quad = 40\%$

How to Calculate Diversity ROI

Finance and accounting personnel may take issue with calculations involving the return on investment for efforts such as diversity initiatives. Nevertheless, the expression is fairly common and conveys an adequate meaning of financial evaluation.

ROI may be calculated prior to a diversity program to estimate the potential cost effectiveness or after a program has been conducted to measure the results achieved. The methods of calculation are the same. However, the estimated return before a program is usually calculated for a proposal to implement the program. The data for its calculation are more subjective and usually less reliable than the data after the program is completed. Because of this factor, management may require a higher ROI for a diversity program in the proposal stage.

DROI Fundamentals

Annualized Values

All of the DROI formulas presented here will use annualized values so that the first year impact of the diversity initiative's investment is developed. Using annualized values is becoming a generally accepted "best practice" for developing DROI in organizations. This approach is a conservative way to develop DROI, since many short-term diversity initiatives have added value in the second or third year. For long-term diversity initiatives, annualized values are inappropriate and longer time frames need to be used.

When selecting the approach to measure DROI, it is important to communicate to the target audience the formula used and the assumptions made to arrive at the decision to use it. This action can avoid misunderstandings and confusion surrounding how the DROI value was actually developed. Although several approaches are described in this chapter, two stand out as the preferred methods—the benefit/cost ratio and the basic DROI formula. These two approaches are described next, along with brief coverage of the other approaches.

Benefit/Cost Ratio

One of the earliest methods for evaluating investments in diversity initiatives is the benefit/costs ratio (read as the benefits-to-costs ratio). This method compares the benefits of the program to the costs in a ratio. In formula form, the ratio is:

BCR = <u>Diversity Initiative Benefits</u>
       Diversity Initiative Costs

In simple terms, the BCR compares the annual economic benefits of the diversity initiative to the cost of the initiative. A BCR of one means that the benefits equal the costs. A BCR of two, usually written as 2:1, indicates that for each dollar spent on the diversity initiative, two dollars were returned as benefits.

The following example will illustrate the use of the benefit/cost ratio. A diversity leadership initiative, designed for managers and supervisors, was implemented at an electric and gas utility. In a follow-up evaluation, action planning and business performance monitoring were used to capture benefits. The first year payoff for the initiative was $1,077,750. The total fully loaded implementation cost was $215,500. Thus, the ratio was:

$$BCR = \frac{\$1,077,750}{\$215,500} = 5:1$$

For every one dollar invested in the diversity initiative, five dollars in benefits were returned.

The principal advantage of using this approach is that it avoids traditional financial measures so that there is no confusion when comparing diversity initiative investments with other investments in the organization. Investments in plants, equipment, or subsidiaries, for example, are not usually evaluated with the benefits/cost method. Some executives prefer not to use the same method to compare the returns in diversity with the returns on other investments.

Consequently, this method for calculating diversity return on investment stands out as a unique type of evaluation.

Unfortunately, there is no standard as to what constitutes an acceptable benefits/cost ratio for diversity. A standard should be established within an organization, perhaps even for a specific type of diversity initiative. However, a 1:1 ratio is unacceptable for most programs, and in some organizations, a 1.25:1 ratio is required, where 1.25 times the cost is the benefit.

The DROI Formula

Perhaps the most appropriate formula for evaluating an investment in a diversity initiative is the net initiative benefits divided by costs. The ratio is usually expressed as a percent where the fractional values are multiplied by 100. In formula form, the DROI formula is expressed as:

$$DROI(\%) = \frac{\text{Net Diversity Initiative Benefits}}{\text{Diversity Initiative Costs}} \times 100$$

Net benefits are diversity initiative benefits minus the diversity initiative costs. The DROI value is related to the BCR by a factor of one. For example, a BCR of 2.45 is the same as a DROI value of 145%. This formula is essentially the same as ROI in other types of investments. For example, when a firm builds a new plant, the ROI is found by dividing annual

How to Calculate Diversity ROI

earnings by the investment. The annual earnings is comparable to net benefits (annual benefits minus the cost). The investment is comparable to the diversity initiative costs, which represent the investment in the initiative.

A DROI on a diversity investment of 50% means that the costs are recovered and an additional 50% of the costs are reported as "earnings". A diversity investment of 150% indicates that the costs have been recovered and an additional 1.5 multiplied by the costs is captured as "earnings." An example illustrates the DROI calculation. Magnavox Electronics Systems Company conducted an 18-week literacy program for entry level electrical and mechanical assemblers (Ford, D, "Three Rs in the Workplace", in "In Action: Measuring Return on Investment", Vol.1, J. Phillips (Ed.), Alexandria, VA: American Society for Training and Development, 1994, pp85-104.) The results of the program were impressive. Productivity and quality alone yielded an annual value of $321,600. The total fully loaded costs for the program were $38,233. Thus, the diversity return on investment becomes:

$$DROI(\%) = \frac{\$321,600 - \$38,233}{\$38,233} \times 100 = 741\%$$

For each dollar invested, Magnavox received $7.4 dollars in return after the cost of the program had been recovered.

Using the DROI formula essentially places diversity investments on a level playing field with other investments using the same formula and similar concepts. Key management and financial executives who regularly use ROI with other investments easily understand the DROI calculation.

While there are no generally accepted standards, some organizations establish a minimum requirement or hurdle rate for an ROI in human resource-based programs such as training. An ROI minimum of 25% is set by some organizations. The same will eventually come true for diversity initiatives. This target value in training is usually above the percentage required for other types of investments. The rationale: the ROI process for training is still relatively new and often involves some subjective input, including estimations. Because of that, a higher standard is required or suggested, with 25% being the desired figure for these organizations. I feel it is mandatory that DROI calculations follow suit.

Other ROI Methods

In addition to the traditional DROI formula previously described, several other measures may be used under the general term of return on investment. These measures are designed primarily for evaluating other types of financial measures, but may offer some alternate possibilities in measuring the return on investments in diversity.

Payback Period

The payback period is a common method for evaluating capital expenditures. With this approach, the annual cash proceeds (savings) produced by an investment are equated to the original cash outlay required by the investment to arrive at some multiple of cash proceeds equal to the original investment. Measurement is usually in terms of years and months. For example, if the cost savings generated from a diversity initiative are constant each year, the payback period is determined by dividing the total original cash investment (development costs, outside program purchases, etc.) by the amount of the expected annual or actual savings. The savings represent the net savings after the diversity initiative's expenses are subtracted. To illustrate this calculation, assume that an initial diversity initiative cost is $100,000 with a three-year useful life. The annual net savings from the diversity initiative are expected to be $40,000. Thus, the payback period becomes:

Payback Period = <u>Total Investment</u>
Annual Savings

Payback Period = $\dfrac{\$100,000}{\$40,000}$ = 2.5 Years

The diversity initiative will "pay back" the original investment in 2.5 years.

The payback period is simple to use, but has the limitation of ignoring the time value of money. It has not enjoyed widespread use in evaluating investments such as training or human resources in general.

Discounted Cash Flow

Discounted cash flow is a method of evaluating investment opportunities in which certain values are assigned to the timing of the proceeds from the investment. The assumption, based on interest rates, is that a dollar earned today is more valuable than a dollar a year from now.

There are several ways of using the discounted cash flow concept to evaluate capital expenditures. The most popular one is probably the net present value of an investment. This approach compares the savings, year by year, with the outflow of cash required by the investment. The expected savings received each year are discounted by selected interest rates. The outflow of cash is also discounted by the same interest rate. If the present value of the savings does exceed the present value of the outlays after discounting at a common interest rate, the investment is usually acceptable in the eyes of management. The discounted cash flow method has the advantage of ranking investments, but it becomes difficult to calculate.

Internal Rate of Return

The internal rate of return (IRR) method determines the interest rate required to make the present value of the cash flow equal to zero. It represents the maximum rate of interest that could be paid if all diversity project funds were borrowed and the organization had to break even on the projects. The IRR considers the time value of money and is unaffected by the scale of the project. It can be used to rank alternatives and can be used to make accept/reject decisions when a minimum rate of return is specified. This can make an investment alternative with a high rate of return look even better than it really is, and a project with a low rate of return look even worse. In practice, the IRR is rarely used to evaluate human resource-based investments.

Utility Analysis

Another interesting approach for developing a diversity initiative's payoff is Utility Analysis. This method has been applied to training initiatives and could be useful for evaluating diversity training initiatives. Utility is a function of the duration of a training program's effect on employee performance, the number of employees trained, the validity of the training program, the value of the jobs affected for which training was provided, and the total program cost (Schmidt, F.L., Hunter, J. E., Pearlman, K, "Assessing the Economic Impact of Personnel Programs on Workforce Productivity," Personnel Psychology, Vol. 35, p.333-347, 1982).

Utility analysis measures the economic contribution of a program according to how effective the program was in identifying and modifying behavior, therefore we would need to examine the future service contribution of employees. Schmidt, Hunter and Pearlman derived the following formula, which I have adapted for assessing the dollar value of a diversity training initiative.

$$\Delta U = T \times N \times dt \times Sdy - N \times C$$

Where:

ΔU = Monetary value of the diversity training initiative

T = Duration in number of years of a diversity training initiative's effects on performance

N = Number of employees trained

dt = True difference in job performance between the average trained and the average untrained employees in units of standard deviation

Sdy = Standard deviation of job performance of the untrained group in dollars

C = Cost of the diversity training initiative per employee

How to Calculate Diversity ROI

Of all the factors in this formula, the true difference in job performance and the value of the target job are the most difficult to develop. The validity is determined by noting the performance differences between trained and untrained employees. The simplest method for obtaining this information is to have supervisors rate the performance of each group. Supervisors and experts also estimate the value of the target job, Sdy.

Utility analysis is based totally on estimations. Because of the subjective nature of this approach, it has not achieved widespread acceptance by diversity, training, or human resource professionals as a practical tool for evaluating the return on investment in human resource-based areas.

Consequences of Not Implementing A Diversity Initiative

For some organizations, the consequences of not implementing a diversity initiative can be very serious. An organization's inability to perform adequately due to real or perceived barriers caused by a poor diversity inclusive climate might mean that it is unable to take on additional business or that it may lose existing business because of a dysfunctional workforce, poor connections with ethnic markets, high turnover, etc. Also, diversity can help an organization avoid serious operational problems (accidents) or non-compliance problems, etc. Measuring the consequences of not implementing a diversity initiative is noteworthy and involves the following steps:

- Establish that there is a potential problem, loss, or opportunity.
- Isolate the problems that lack of performance may create such as non-compliance issues, loss of business, or the inability to take on additional business.
- Develop an estimate of the potential value of the problem, loss or opportunity.
- If other factors are involved, determine the impact of each factor on the loss of income.
- Estimate the total cost of the diversity initiative using the techniques described in this book.
- Compare the benefits with costs.

This approach has also some disadvantages. The potential loss of income can be highly subjective and difficult to measure. Also, it may be difficult to isolate the factors involved and to determine their weight relative to lost income. Because of these concerns, this approach to evaluating the diversity return on investment is limited to certain types of initiatives, programs, or situations.

How to Calculate Diversity ROI

DROI Issues to Consider

DROI Complexity

Developing the return on investment in diversity is a complex issue. This book was designed to take the complex process of diversity measurement and diversity return on investment concepts and simplify them by breaking them down into small steps so it is understandable, practical and acceptable to a variety of audiences. The diagram shown below can represent this complexity. The sheer number of possibilities that can be created if we only recognize and use 10 methods under each heading make the DROI process complex:

The Complexity of Calculating DROI

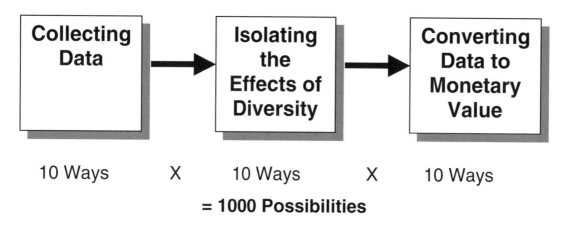

This graphic underscores the important advantage of using a combination of methods. With so many different ways to tackle these three critical issues, the DROI process can be applied to almost any type of diversity initiative.

Cautions When Using DROI

Because of the complexity and sensitivity of the DROI process, caution is needed when developing, calculating, and communicating the return on investment. The implementation of the DROI process is a very important issue, and is a goal of many diversity organizations. Addressing the following issues can help make certain the process does not go off track.

The DROI process should be develop for an initiative where a serious needs assessment has been conducted. Because of the evaluation problems that can develop when it is not clear that a need exists, it is recommended that the DROI study be conducted with initiatives that have had a comprehensive needs assessment. However, I am well aware that in some cases practical considerations and management requests may prohibit this suggested requirement.

The DROI analysis should always include one or more strategies for isolating the effects of the diversity initiative. Because of the importance of accounting for the influences of other factors, this step in the process must not be ignored. Too often, an excellent study—from what appears to be a very successful diversity effort—is perceived to be worthless because there was no attempt to account for other factors. Omission of this step seriously diminishes the credibility of the diversity initiative study.

When making estimates, use the most reliable and credible sources. Because estimates are critical to any type of analysis, they will usually be an important part of a DROI study. When they are used, they should be developed properly and obtained from the most reliable and credible sources—those individuals who best understand the overall situation and can provide accurate estimates.

Take a conservative approach when developing both benefits and costs. Conservatism in DROI analysis builds accuracy and credibility. What matters most is how the target audience perceives the value of the data. A conservative approach is always recommended for both the numerator of the DROI formula (diversity initiative benefits) and the denominator (diversity initiative costs).

Use caution when comparing the ROI in diversity with other financial returns. There are many ways to calculate the return on funds invested or assets employed. The ROI is just one of them. Although the calculation for DROI uses the same basic formula as in other investment evaluations, it may not be fully understood by the target group. Its calculation method and its meaning should be clearly communicated. More importantly, it should be an item accepted by management as an appropriate measure for measuring diversity results. This kind of credibility must be earned by taking the time to complete all of the assessment and measurement steps in the process.

Involve management in developing the return.
Management ultimately makes the decision if a DROI value is acceptable. To the extent possible, management should be involved in setting parameters for calculations and establishing targets by which diversity initiatives are considered acceptable within the organization.

Approach sensitive and controversial issues with caution. Occasionally, sensitive and controversial issues will be generated when discussing a DROI value. It is best to avoid debates over what is measurable and what is not measurable unless there is clear evidence of the issue in question. The issue can be included in the overall measurement process as an intangible benefit. Also, some initiatives are so fundamental to the organization's survival that any attempt to measure them is unnecessary. For example, a diversity initiative designed to improve customer service in a customer-focused organization may escape the scrutiny of a DROI evaluation, on the assumption that if the initiative is well designed, it will improve customer service. As more organizations implement DROI studies and standards evolve, the diversity measurement discipline will have increasing evidence that DROI values can be trusted with accuracy and validity.

Develop case studies of your DROI calculations. Creating case studies of your DROI studies can help educate your organization on the full value of your efforts and the benefits in measuring diversity results. These successes and learning opportunities can help other diversity initiatives and other diversity personnel throughout the organization. Hubbard & Hubbard, Inc. offers specific workshops designed to help you develop or turn your existing data into a diversity business case study.

Do not boast about a high return. It is not unusual to generate what appears to be a very high DROI for a diversity initiative. This can open the diversity organization up to undue criticism and scrutiny even when the numbers are an accurate reflection of the facts. The value for DROI will be built as more members of the organization come to understand the processes through their own participation on diversity initiative teams and obvious improvements in organizational climate and performance.

Do not try to use DROI on every diversity initiative. Some diversity initiatives are difficult to quantify, and a DROI calculation may not be feasible. Other methods of presenting the benefits may be more appropriate. It is helpful to set specific criteria for the selection of diversity initiatives that will be evaluated when using the DROI level of analyses.

Identifying and Incorporating Intangible Measures

Importance of Recognizing Intangible Measures in Diversity

Not all measures can or should be converted to monetary values. By design, some are captured and reported as intangible measures. Although they may not be perceived as valuable as the measures converted to monetary values, intangible measures are critical to the overall evaluation process. In some diversity initiatives such as diversity leadership training, managing multicultural conflict, etc., the intangible, or non-monetary benefits can be more important than monetary or tangible measures. Consequently, these measures should be monitored and reported as part of the overall evaluation. In practice, every diversity initiative, regardless of its nature, scope, and content, will have intangible measures associated with it. The challenge is to efficiently identify and report them. Some of the more typical variables that are referred to as "intangible" include the following:

Typical Intangible Variables Linked with Diversity	
■ Attitude Survey Data	■ Employee Transfers
■ Organizational Commitment	■ Customer Satisfaction Survey Data
■ Climate Survey Data	■ Customer Complaints
■ Employee Complaints	■ Customer Response Time
■ Grievances	■ Teamwork
■ Discrimination Complaints	■ Cooperation
■ Stress Reduction	■ Conflict
■ Employee Turnover	■ Decisiveness
■ Employee Absenteeism	■ Communication
■ Employee Tardiness	■ Etc.

The good news is that with the advent of processes such as causal pathway analysis, and staple measurement processes such as correlation, linear and multiple regression, and even cross-tab correlation, we are pinpointing diversity contributions in many of the so-called "intangible" areas and converting diversity initiative contributions into monetary values. Nonetheless, if you need to report these variables as intangibles, then the following procedures will help.

Identification of Measures

Intangible measures can be identified in several ways representing different time frames. First, they can be uncovered early in the process, during the needs assessment. Once identified, the tangible data are planned for collection as part of the overall data collection strategy. For example, a multicultural marketing training for team leaders program has several hard data measures linked to the effort. An intangible measure, employee satisfaction, is identified and monitored with no plans to convert it to a monetary value. Thus, from the beginning, this measure is destined to be a non-monetary benefit reported along with the DROI results.

A second way in which an intangible benefit is identified is to discuss with the sponsors or management what is the impact of the diversity initiative as they see it. They can usually identify intangible measures that are expected to be influenced by the diversity initiative.

The third way in which an intangible measure is identified is during an attempt to convert the data to monetary values. If the process used to convert the data to monetary value loses credibility, the measure should be reported as an intangible benefit. For example, in a multicultural selling skills program, customer satisfaction is identified early in the initiative as one of the measures of the diversity initiative's success. A conversion to monetary values was attempted. However, the process of assigning a value to the data lost credibility, therefore, customer satisfaction was reported as an intangible. Currently, to remedy this problem, correlation's can be made linking customer satisfaction to customer retention and then customer retention to dollars to calculate the benefits in hard dollar amounts.

The fourth way in which an intangible measure is identified is during a follow-up evaluation. Although the measure was neither expected nor anticipated in the initial diversity initiative design, the measure surfaces on a questionnaire, in an interview, or during a focus group. Questions are often asked about other improvements linked to the diversity initiative. Several intangible measures are usually provided and there are no planned attempts to place a value on the actual measure. For example, in a diverse customer service initiative, participants were asked specifically what had improved about their work area and their relationship with customers as a result of the application of the skills they acquired in the diversity initiative. The participants provided over a dozen intangible measures, which managers perceived to be linked directly with the diversity initiative.

Application Exercise

1. List the intangible benefits associated with the diversity initiative you cited in the last Application Exercise.

What to Do Next

_____

_____

_____

2. If you had to estimate the value of these intangible benefits and annualize the dollar value, what would it be?

For most intangible data, no specific analysis is planned. Previous attempts to convert intangible data to monetary units resulted in aborting the entire process; therefore, no further data analysis was conducted. Now new processes are available to use on this type of data. This step is necessary when there is a need to know the specific amount of change in the intangible measure that is linked to the initiative. In many cases, however, the intangible data reflect improvement. Since the value of this data is not placed in the DROI calculation, intangible measures are not normally used to justify additional diversity initiatives or continuation of an existing initiative. Consequently, a detailed analysis is not needed. Intangible benefits are viewed as supporting evidence of the diversity initiative's success and should be presented as qualitative data.

How to Calculate Diversity ROI

Step 6 – Report It to Others

Step 6 – Report It to Others

Introduction

Once you have an understanding of the processes necessary to identify diversity costs and benefits and the tools to calculate the DROI impact, you are ready to develop a communications strategy to report it to others. This strategy includes elements such as:

➢ Considering some general principles for reporting statistical data and results to others

➢ Creating a Management Summary

➢ Communicating Background Information regarding the diversity research study

➢ Describing the Evaluation Strategy

➢ Discussing the Data Collection, Analysis and Performance Tracking plan

➢ Detailing the diversity Initiative's Costs, and Benefits

➢ Profiling an Initiative's Results and DROI Impact

➢ Identifying your Conclusions and Recommendations

How to Calculate Diversity ROI

General Reporting Principles

Reporting the results is almost as important as producing results. It will do you and your department little good if you are making great progress and few people know about it. In effect, you must become a cheerleader and chief advocate for your diversity efforts. Regardless of the message, a few general principles are important when communicating your diversity initiative's results:

- The communication must be timely
- The communication should be targeted to specific audiences
- The media should be carefully selected
- The communication should be unbiased and always modest
- The communication must be consistent
- Testimonials are more effective if they are from individuals with audience credibility
- The audience's perception of the Diversity Department will influence communication strategy

The communication must be timely - Usually, diversity initiative results should be communicated as soon as they are known and are packaged for presentation. From a practical standpoint however, it may be best to delay the communication to a convenient time, such as the next edition of the newsletter or the next general staff meeting. Several questions about timing must be addressed.

- Is the audience prepared for the information, considering the content and other events?
- Are they expecting it?
- When is the best time to have maximum impact on the audience?

The communication should be targeted to specific audiences - The communication will be more efficient when it is designed for a specific group. The message can be specifically tailored to the interests, needs and expectations of the group. The length, content, details, and slant will vary with the audience.

The media should be carefully selected - For a specific group, one medium may be more effective than others. Face-to-face meetings may be better with some groups than special bulletins. A memo to top management may be more effective than an evaluation report. The selection of an appropriate medium will help improve the effectiveness of the process.

The communication should be unbiased and always modest - Facts must be separated from fiction, and accurate statements must replace opinions. Some target audiences may view communication from the Diversity Department with skepticism and may look for biased information and opinions. Boastful statements will sometimes turn off individuals, and most of the content of the communication will be lost. Observable, believable facts carry more weight than extreme, sensational claims, although the claims may be needed to get initial attention.

The communication must be consistent - The timing and the content of the communication should be consistent with past practices. A special communication at an unusual time may create suspicion when a particular group, such as top management, regularly receives communication, the information should continue even if the results are not good. If selected results are omitted, it might leave the impression that only good results are reported.

Testimonials are more effective if they are from individuals with audience credibility - Attitudes are strongly influenced by others, particularly by those who are admired and respected. Testimonials about the diversity initiative results, when solicited from individuals who are generally respected in the organization can have a strong impact on the effectiveness of the message. This respect may be earned from leadership ability, position, special skills, or knowledge. The opposite of this principle is true. A testimonial from an individual who commands little respect and is regarded as a poor performer can have a negative impact.

The audience's perception of the diversity organization will influence communication strategy - Perceptions are difficult to change. A negative opinion of the Diversity organization may not be changed by the mere presentation of facts. However, the presentation of facts alone may strengthen the opinion of individuals who already have a favorable impression of the department. It provides reassurance that their support is appropriate. The department's credibility should be an important consideration when developing an overall communications strategy. A Diversity organization with low credibility may have problem when trying to be persuasive in a communication. Nonetheless, communicating significant diversity results can have a positive effect on increasing the credibility of the department.

Key Questions to Answer when Selecting the Message

In order for your diversity initiative report to have the maximum impact, you must answer a few key questions:

➢ Is the audience interested in the subject?
➢ Do they really want to hear the information?
➢ Is the timing right for this audience?
➢ Is this audience familiar with the views of the Diversity

organization?

➤ How do they prefer to have results communicated?

➤ Are they likely to find the results threatening?

➤ What else is happening in the organization that may compete for their attention to focus on the diversity results?

➤ Which medium will be most convincing to this group?

To be an effective communicator, you must get to know the audience you will be working with noting how others have been successful in reporting data to them in the past. Find out what information is needed and why. Try to understand each audience's point of view - some may want to see the results while others may not. Others may be neutral. Keep in mind that your reporting approach must reach every one in a way the helps them understand the significance of the work you have completed.

Now that you understand some of the rules for reporting your diversity results, let's examine the components to create the diversity evaluation report.

Developing the Evaluation Report

The type of formal evaluation report used to communicate results depends on the amount of detailed information that is developed for various target audiences. In general, the objective is to keep the presentation to 1-2 pages. For senior leadership groups, it should be condensed in a management summary or briefing. For other audiences, the evaluation report can be "layered" into sections such that you present those portions that are most applicable to your target audience.

The following elements should be covered in a complete diversity evaluation report:

➢ Management Summary
➢ Background Information
➢ Evaluation Strategy
➢ Data Collection, Analysis and Performance Tracking
➢ Diversity Initiative's Costs, and Benefits
➢ Diversity Initiative Results and DROI Calculations
➢ Conclusions and Recommendations

Management Summary

The Management Summary gives a brief synopsis of the diversity measurement study, the approaches used and the conclusions and recommendations you would like to make based upon the findings. Its basic purpose is to:

■ Provide a brief overview of the entire report
■ Explain significant conclusions and recommendations

It is usually written last and appears first in the report. Another typical writing convention is that it is usually one page in length.

Background Information

Next, the Background Information section does exactly what it says…provides background information. In this section you introduce the need for the diversity measurement study and its links to the organization's strategic business objectives. Its basic purpose is to:

- Provide a general description of the events leading to the creation of the diversity initiative

- Describe the Diversity Business Rationale that links the study to the organization's strategic business objectives. This can be obtained from the needs analysis and the diversity strategic plan

- Discuss specific issues and events critical to the development and implementation of the diversity measurement effort

This section explains the basic foundation that makes this study valuable to the organization.

Evaluation Strategy

The Evaluation Strategy section outlines the statistical analysis plan that was used during the study. Its basic purpose is to:

- Describe all of the components that made up the total evaluation process

- Explain in detail the purpose of the diversity evaluation effort

- Describe the data collection techniques and presents them as exhibits

- Identify other Information related to the design, timing, responsibilities of personnel and the execution of the evaluation.

This allows the target audience to understand the framework that made the study possible.

Data Collection, Analysis and Performance Tracking

The Data Collection, Analysis and Performance Tracking section explains how the data was collected, what occurred during the implementation of the analysis methods, and outlines the techniques and methods used to track the diversity initiative's performance based upon key assessments taken.

This section usually presents the data collected in both raw and finished formats. And, it illustrates what measures were used that require special explanations. Converted monetary values are discussed along with the methods of data analysis and appropriate explanations and interpretations

How to Calculate Diversity ROI

Diversity Initiative Costs and Benefits

This section explains the how the costs and benefits were captured or determined. Its basic purpose is to:

- Summarize costs by examining each cost component
- Show costs as they relate to analysis, development, implementation expenses, maintenance, and evaluation efforts
- Discuss assumptions made in estimating costs

It is important to note that there is no need to explain the complete system for assigning and allocating cost. A footnote to explain that a description of the system is available from the diversity department is sufficient

Initiative Results and DROI Calculations

This is the section of the Evaluation Report that your audience will want to discuss in detail. It is the section that should be crafted to appeal to the informational needs of each audience member. This suggests that if you are presenting in a meeting room, this section should be supported with visual graphics, sound and movement to illustrate the impact of the results such that you appeal to all learning styles—visual, auditory and kinesthetics. This section is probably the most important part of the report. Its basic purpose is to:

- Present a summary of the results with charts, diagrams, tables, and other visual aids.

- Where possible, include a cost/benefit analysis along with the DROI calculation (DROI= Net Initiative Benefits/Initiative Costs) and the Benefit/Cost ratio (BCR = Initiative Benefits/Initiative Costs
- Outline various program benefits
- Present a complete picture of both hard and soft data

Conclusions and Recommendations

Finally, the Conclusions and Recommendations section brings the Evaluation Report to a close. Its basic purpose is to:

- Present conclusions based upon an analysis of all information
- Give a brief explanation explaining how the conclusions were derived
- Discuss the impact of conclusions on the successful operation of the organization
- Present a list of recommendations including changes in the diversity initiative approach or changes to other systems within the organization

It is critical that the conclusions and recommendations are fully consistent with the findings described in the previous sections of the diversity evaluation report.

While these components are key parts of a complete Diversity Evaluation Report, the report can be scaled down, as necessary to provide needed documentation to meet target audience needs.

Communicating Results to a Variety of Audiences

While several potential audiences could receive the DROI study, four audiences should always receive the data. A senior management team (however defined) should always receive information about the DROI project because of their interest in the process and their influence to allocate additional resources for diversity and the measurement of its impact. The supervisors of the initiative's participants need to have the DROI information so they will continue to support other diversity measurement efforts and reinforce specific behaviors and methods suggested in the diversity initiative for performance improvement. The participants in the diversity initiative who actually achieved results should receive a summary of the DROI information so they understand what the entire group accomplished. This also reinforces their commitment to make the process work. The diversity staff must understand the DROI process and, consequently, need to receive the DROI study information. In addition, other groups may receive information based on the type of diversity measurement initiative conducted and the other potential audiences.

Other Means to Communicate Diversity Results

In addition to communicating the results of your diversity

initiative measurement study using an evaluation report, there are other methods available. These methods include:

- Staff Meetings
- Supervisor/Leader Meetings
- Panel Discussions
- Management Clubs and Associations
- Annual "State of the Company" Meetings
- Company or Diversity Newsletters
- General Interest Publications - Human interest stories, participant recognition, annual reports
- Brochures/Booklets/Pamphlets/Recruiting Brochures/Special Achievements/Success Stories

What to Do Next

Application Exercise

1. Who was/is the key audience this diversity initiative?

_____

_____

2. What were/are they most concerned about?

_____

_____

_____

3. What method did/will you use to communicate the DROI results? Why this method?

_____

_____

_____

Reporting Your Results Should Not Be An Afterthought

Reporting your diversity measurement results is critical to the total evaluation process. It should not be left as an afterthought simply because you are achieving the intended results. These results have to be communicated in a conservative tone and effective manner to demonstrate and maintain diversity's link to the business bottom-line. Your goal must be to communicate diversity results in facts, figures and financials that make the business case for performance!

Step 7 – Track and Assess Progress

Step 7 – Track and Assess Progress

Introduction

Tracking and assessing the overall progress of your diversity ROI initiative is critical for institutionalizing any gains achieved in the process. A tracking system is usually made up of the documents and procedures you used to collect and summarize the data for feedback purposes. Although it is an often overlooked part of the process, an effective diversity measurement tracking and monitoring plan can help keep your diversity initiatives on target and let others know what progress is being made for the organization. By using diversity return on investment (DROI) techniques, you can establish your diversity efforts on a solid business foundation like any other organizational initiative.

What Does a Good Tracking System Look Like?

An effective tracking system is one that is:

Relevant – The organization receives information directly related to the diversity measures and metrics being used.

Frequent – Generally, the more frequent the feedback on key items the better. The goal is to provide feedback often enough to prevent the organization from drifting off the diversity and business performance target.

Immediate – Feedback should come as soon as possible after work is completed or on a regularly scheduled basis once processes are placed in an implementation mode.

Specific – Feedback should state exactly how the organization did in accomplishing the diversity initiative's goals and objectives. This includes meeting any Benefit-to-Cost ratio (BCR) and Diversity Return on Investment (DROI) targets as well as stories of success (anecdotal) achieved along the way.

Remember: "You can't manage what you don't measure" and "you can't know if you are making progress if you are not tracking the diversity results to compare". Unless the organization knows how it is doing in meeting its diversity initiative targets, it can't improve. Honest, two-way communication between the diversity implementation team and the organization begins with accurate data about how well the organization is performing relative to meeting its diversity goals and objectives. Without it, both the diversity implementation team and management can only exchange subjective opinions about how the diversity initiatives have performed.

Monitoring Your DROI Initiative's Progress

The initial implementation schedule of the DROI study provides a variety of key events or milestones. Routine progress reports need to be developed to present the status and progress of these diversity initiative events and their key milestones. Reports are usually developed at six-month intervals, however, they can be more frequent depending on the informational needs of your audience. Two target audiences, the diversity organization staff and senior managers, are critical for progress reporting. The entire Human Resources and operations communities within the organization should be kept informed on the initiative's progress. In addition, senior managers need to know the extent to which the diversity return on investment study is being implemented and how it is working in the organization. To maintain this level of information and reporting capability, automated systems may be necessary.

MetricLINK^{tm} an Automated Diversity Measurement System for Tracking Improved Performance

Developing diversity measurement strategies, business objectives and tactics, calculating formulas for diversity metrics, keeping everyone informed on the diversity initiative's progress, etc., can be tedious work. Someone must take the responsibility to develop procedures and a method to systematically monitor and track each diversity measure and set of metrics used to implement the initiative, then summarize the results over time. This is a task that is best done by a computer or an automated measurement system.

As I stated earlier, there's a saying that goes "If you don't measure it, you can't control it. And, if you can't control it, you can't manage it." MetricLink^{tm}, a comprehensive diversity strategy alignment and performance-tracking tool developed and distributed by Hubbard & Hubbard, Inc., Petaluma, California, has been found to be an easy-to-use, highly effective measurement planning, analysis and reporting system that provides all the information you need to "manage-by-facts". It integrates and organizes diversity measures and strategies all in one place.

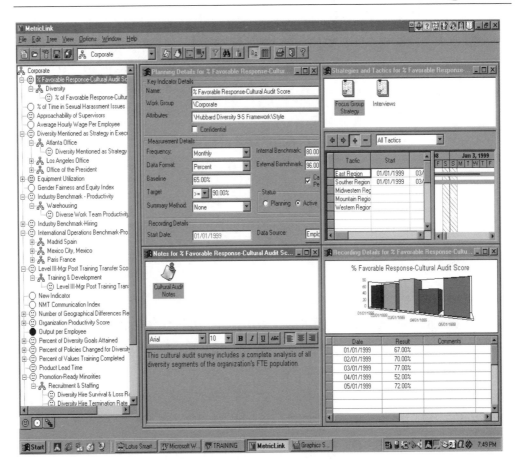

The system frees the diversity professional up from some of the time-consuming tasks of tracking, calculating and reporting a diversity initiative's results.

Some of the benefits of MetricLink^{tm} are:

➤ Aligns diversity measures with strategic business objectives and the organization's operations structure.

➤ Multiple views allow diversity measures to be reviewed in different contexts.

How to Calculate Diversity ROI

➤ "Drill-down" capabilities are available to view diversity measures by component, by location, by workgroup, or by results area.

➤ Multiple comparisons of actual diversity initiative performance to organizational targets stretch goals, historical performance, benchmarks, or other reference points is available.

➤ You can vary target specifications over multiple periods to reflect changing objectives over time.

➤ "*Weights*", performance scaling, and diversity initiative indexing capabilities can be used to combine several measures into meaningful summary values.

➤ Color-coded reporting allows you to easily monitor performance "*at a glance*".

➤ Team or individual ownership can be assigned for each diversity measure promoting accountability and communication.

➤ Customized reporting and printout capabilities are available.

➤ The Notes, Task and Project planning features are "*built-in*" to capture ideas and actions for diversity and organizational performance improvement.

➤ Easy-to-use menus and icons to intuitively locate features and functions with a "*point and click*".

Using the MetricLINK^{tm} approach, no programming is required and typical administrator training only takes about 4 hours to get you up and running on the system. MetricLINK^{tm} software options allow the use of diversity measurement templates for key diversity benchmark measures you can use immediately. Setup and the "ready to use" timeframe is less than a day if standard measures are used and organization specific measures are ready and well defined. MetricLINK^{tm} offers options to run on a stand-alone Personal Computer (PC) Lap or Desktop) or using the Network option, MetricLINK^{tm} can be networked with up to 100 users anywhere in the world.

Survey Pro^{tm}: A Timesaving Survey Development Tool

Survey Pro^{tm} is a great companion measurement tool to MetricLINK^{tm}. Also distributed by Hubbard & Hubbard, Inc., Survey Pro^{tm} is an all-in-one survey development software package that takes the guesswork out of assembling survey questionnaires of any kind using a fast, and easy-to-use process. Survey Pro^{tm}'s flexible and powerful tools are designed to suit any application, making survey development quick and cost effective. For survey design, Survey Pro^{tm} quickly generates polished layouts for paper or internet forms.

Survey Pro^{tm} can help you accomplish the following tasks:

➤ Develop survey questionnaires

➤ Gather answers from respondents

➤ Organize responses for graphical reporting using a wide variety of layouts such as summary tables, pie charts, bar charts, 3-D charts, stacked bar charts, comparison profile graphs, X-Y plots, written comment summaries, and much more

➤ Present conclusions

➤ Monitor and compare changes in the data

Survey Pro^{tm} operates very quickly due to its library of common measurement scales which requires you to simply enter your customized question text. Or you can design your own scales. Survey Pro^{tm} can accommodate up to 500 scales and 2000 questions in each survey file. This product makes developing and analyzing survey data as part of a DROI study a breeze!

Other Measurement Software Options

Other measurement software options include using popular spreadsheet programs such as Microsoft Excel, Lotus 1-2-3, etc., and project management software programs such as Microsoft Project, as well as using data base management programs such as Microsoft Access or Lotus Approach. These software solutions will however require you to design and program formula calculations, recording and data input elements to track and monitor your progress. Additional automation options could include a formal software development process using your Management Information Systems (MIS) organization. No matter what system you choose, it must allow you to respond quickly and effectively with up-to-the-minute information regarding the status of your diversity initiatives. Tracking and assessing your progress as the diversity initiative matures must become a routine, integral part of your system of measurement.

Institutionalizing Your Diversity Measurement System

Institutionalizing the diversity measurement tracking and monitoring process is a three-part challenge:

➤ Creating and refining the DROI process and other measurement systems that supports it; Managers themselves must be instrumental in helping to create the measurement model and align with it. This helps to create buy-in.

How to Calculate Diversity ROI

➤ Creating management alignment around the use of the DROI measurement model to run the organization; and,

➤ Deploying the DROI measurement model so as to build business literacy and trust among everyone that participates in or is affected by these measurement methods.

First, it is important to build alignment around the DROI measurement process and its techniques: The DROI model and its measures (Survival and Loss Rates, Stability, Instability Factors, BCR, DROI calculations, % of Favorable Responses, etc.) make up a single system. This system must become a cornerstone for management decision-making. Therefore every manager, especially those at the top must understand the system and buy into it.

Second, it is essential to deploy the diversity measurement system properly in order to create a sense of ownership among employees and staff. This is more than simple communications.

Thirdly, it is a task of building trust and financial literacy among employees about the numbers and diversity metrics that drive the business. Unless employees grasp the purpose of the system, understand the economics of the organization and industry, and have a clear picture of how their own work fits into the "diversity value chain", the organization will never succeed in making the whole system work to leverage diversity for performance improvement.

What to Do Next

Application Exercise

1. How did/will you track and assess your progress? Did you use an electronic measurement tracking and survey development system?

_____

_____

_____

2. What follow-up and Monitoring system was/would you put in place?

_____

_____

_____

Importance of Institutionalizing Diversity Measurement and Tracking

Institutionalizing diversity is a key business strategy for reaping the benefits of a diverse workforce. It is one thing to have diversity in your workforce. Its quite another to "utilize" diversity as a competitive advantage. To become an "employer of choice" and to meet key competitive realities of the future, the use of diversity for performance improvement and return on investment must become mandatory.

Building a Financial Performance Mindset

Building a Financial Performance Mindset

Introduction

The business case and rationale for diversity must be linked to strategic business objectives. In addition, diversity initiative results must be displayed and communicated in financial terms. To do this effectively, it requires a financial performance mindset that integrates diversity with other key business strategies that get measured on a regular basis.

Why aren't practitioners doing this now? One study seems to have a few answers. In the Fall, 1998 issue of the Diversity Factor Magazine, Margaret Blackburn White, Editor, asked a group of diversity professionals "if their organizations are demanding evidence that their investments in diversity are paying off on the bottom-line". The answers received suggested that the response landscape is varied. There are few demands for diversity to "justify its existence" by documenting a direct return-on-investment link. However, there was agreement that there is a lot of general conversation about the diversity return-on-investment topic. As competitive pressures, globalization, and other issues become more prevalent, measuring diversity results will become a critical requirement for the future. Customers, shareholders and employees will no longer accept "business as usual".

Remember, diversity management is a process of planning for, organizing, directing and supporting the collective mixtures in organizations (that is, things like race, gender, learning styles, technical expertise, cross functional team behaviors, etc.) in a way that adds value to organizational performance. At a macro level, the 'A-B-C's for measuring diversity management's contribution can be demonstrated by using a six-step measurement tool I developed call the "Diversity Management Contribution Model[tm]". It creates a 30,000-foot view of diversity as a dollars and cents issue to gain management's attention. To illustrate the use of this model, let's create a business setting that requires its use.

Building a Financial Mindset Using the Diversity Management Contribution Model

Let's suppose that you have a meeting with your senior leadership team next Friday and they have asked you to be prepared to talk about the organization's diversity initiatives and any key issues. You have attended these meetings before and presented the business case for diversity, however you have never really used financial approaches for making the case. Recently, you attended a Hubbard &

Building a Financial Performance Mindset

Hubbard, Inc. "Measuring Diversity Results" Workshop and learned, among other things, an approach to get management's attention to the issues using numbers. As you review and prepare your meeting presentation strategy you review the process. Using this model, there are five prerequisites and six steps.

Prerequisites

1. Review your organization's definition of diversity and the its values and vision statements. Make a poster size copy of each to post on the wall of the meeting room.

2. Next, you must fully understand and have in your mind a model of how your organization does business. What are its products, services, and customer markets. That is, who supplies the organization with its raw goods, how are they processed, and who, where, and when are they sold. You must know how the organization makes money and should be familiar with key operations issues, etc. In essence, if you want to connect diversity to the business, you must know how the business operates. Answer the question: "What key organizational issues keep your senior leadership team up at night?" "What problems can diversity help them solve?"

3. Ask the participants attending the meeting to bring their day-timers or calendars that reflect issues they or their staffs have had to handle in the last 3-4 weeks.

4. Review the steps of the Diversity Management Contribution Model[tm]

5. Bring a calculator.

Once you have the prerequisites completed, you are ready to implement the Diversity Contribution Model[tm] approach. Start your presentation by explaining its purpose and briefly review the organization's vision, values, and diversity definition. Make certain you present some examples of the organization's diversity and its application to performance as you review the statement (such as working styles, thinking styles, bi-lingual customer service or marketing representatives servicing ethnic markets, etc.). Use the group's diversity in some of the examples where possible.

Next, ask the group to review their day-timers or calendars for the last 3-4 weeks and list the types of issues they or their staffs dealt with in meetings, with customers, with the community, related to production, sales, marketing, personal or departmental conflicts, etc. Chart these on an easel pad and post them. Summarize the list by examining them for links to your organization's diversity definition and/or the organization's values statement.

Next, ask the group, "What real or perceived barriers seem to get in the way of employees doing their absolute personal best work?" Give examples and relate these to the issues of diversity. Next, connect them to the stated vision and values of the organization. Include things such as issues of respectful treatment by managers and co-workers, having their ideas used, being included in succession and promotion plans, given access to key information, trust, stereotyping, prejudice, discrimination, feeling valued, being seen as capable, etc. Chart the group's responses on an easel pad.

Finally, ask the group the following question which starts the Diversity Management Contribution Model process; "*What percentage of an average 8 hour day is* **NOT SPENT** *on sales, marketing, production, etc. (in other words, mission critical work) due to real or perceived barriers in the workplace?*" If necessary, refer back to the list on the wall or easel pad. Gather example percentages and list them on the chart as participants call them out. Once the frequency of responses die down, take the lowest percent or the number mentioned most frequently and complete the following six steps. (Note: often in senior leadership groups, they may say it doesn't have any impact (0%). If this happens, ask them to think of the first level employees, then answer this question from their point of view).

Insert the percentage into the calculation's first step. For the sake of this example, I will use 25% as my figure, with an average wage of $12/hour, and a 5,000-person organization. To annualize the number, I will use 260 workdays in the year (2080 hours = 260 days which is the equivalent of a 40 hour work week with 2 weeks of vacation per year).

Translating Diversity into Financial Terms

Step	Calculation	Description
1	25% x 8 hours = 2 hours per day per person	This calculation uses the estimate taken from the participants and multiplies by 8 hours.
2	2 hours x $12 per hour = $24 per day per person	The result from step 1 is multiplied by the average wage of all employees. A conservative figure is used.
3	$24 x 5,000 people = $120,000 per day	The result of step 2 is multiplied by the total number of people in the organization (FTEs).
4	$120,000 x 260 days = $31.2 Million per year	The result of step 3 is multiplied by 260 days to annualize the number.
5	$31.2 Million x 45% contribution = $ 14.04 Million	The participant is asked to estimate, "On a scale of 0% contribution to this $31.2 Million to 100% contribution, what amount of this number is attributable to diversity related issues" (review chart). Next, the result of step 4 is multiplied by the % selected.
6	$14.04 Million x 85% confidence factor = $11.9 Million	Finally, the participant is asked, "To ensure an estimate of error, on a scale of 0% confident of this 45% estimate to 100% confident of this estimate, how confident are you of this estimate?" Next, the result of step 5 is multiplied by this estimated percentage.

Building a Financial Performance Mindset

By the time you reach step six, you have the senior leadership team talking about diversity management in financial terms. Many of them will be surprised at the size of the dollar figure. You can mention the following things to help them get an even bigger picture:

- We used the lowest percentage. Others may have been higher.
- We used $12/hour. Some people make more than this amount.
- We pay people for 8 hours worked, not 6 hours, therefore, this is real money sunk as a lost opportunity cost.
- This estimate did not include benefits, bonuses and other perks
- This does not include people taking "mental health" days because the stress is too much, or interviewing for another job on sick leave time.
- If they would like a more accurate number than an estimate, ask them to let you survey employees and ask this question and in focus groups to see what percentage they come up with. (In my experience, this has always resulted in a higher numbers than given by management).

You might ask a question like "If you had this kind of financial loss in Marketing, Sales, Operations, etc., would this issue be important enough to get it on track and obtain the best possible return on investment?" "What if 50-60% of this loss could be turned around and put back into productivity, creativity, innovation, etc.?" Finally, if the group believes this amount is reasonable to lose and the cost will be incurred no matter what, you could always mention that since they see this as a write-off, put the dollars in your diversity budget for next year!

A Causal Model for Understanding a Diversity Management Climate

In addition to using tools such as the "Diversity Management Contribution Model[tm]", diversity practitioners must have a fundamental knowledge of how performance is created in organizations. Good performance and poor performance has a structure, dimensions, elements, and other causal factors that produce the results achieved. If diversity is be tied to and integrated with the business, then it behooves diversity practitioners to know how business is created and what drives performance.

What is Organizational Climate and Diversity Climate?

To aid in this understanding, I developed the "Causal Model of Diversity Climate, Performance and Results[tm]". It provides a basic understanding of the "*performance creation process*" with a specific focus on the manager's role in producing a high performance climate for a diverse workforce. This model is an adaptation of earlier work completed by Harvard professors Dr. George H. Litwin and Dr. Robert A. Stringer in their seminal work on the identification of causal factors, which produce individual motivation and an effective organizational climate. This model was expanded and refined further in later research completed by Dr. Edward E. Hubbard in his doctoral dissertation.

The notion of organizational climate is derived from the weather metaphor, it is the "atmosphere of the workplace," or the answer to the question of "what is it like to work here?" "Diversity climate" I am defining as the "atmosphere of valuing, managing, and utilizing differences similarities in the workplace", or the answer to the question "what is it like to work here as a person with differences or where differences are not applied in task accomplishment?" It is a complex mixture of feelings, perceptions, expectations, norms, values, policies, and procedures that summarize the statements of "the way we do things around here when differences are involved" – it is, in effect over time, the "culture" of the organization.

More formally, organizational climate can be described as the relatively enduring properties of the organization's internal environment which:

➤ Differentiate (usually) one workplace from another

➢ Are related to, but distinct from, the more "objective" properties of the workplace (such as size, structure, job design, etc.)

➢ Are perceived, and experienced, either directly or indirectly by individuals

➢ Can be described, and measured, in fairly specific terms by questioning individuals or observing the flow of work behavior

➢ Influence individuals' motivation and behavior on the job, and;

➢ Can be changed through conscious, and direct, management.

In effect, the concept of climate attempts to capture the complex and multi-faceted transactions occurring between individuals and the organization in which he or she works.

Why is Diversity Climate Important?

Climate is an important managerial concept and practical tool because measures of climate are highly related to "bottom-line" performance measures which managers care about such as sales growth, efficiency measures, productivity indices, and customer perceptions of service quality. We also know that managers themselves can, and do, greatly influence the development of patterns in the organization's climate through their style and practices.

Building a Financial Performance Mindset

Climate affects individuals and organizational performance by arousing the motivated behavior of individuals. In addition, the assessment of climate provides management a "reading" of how well the various aspects of the organization (e.g., technology, strategy planning, organization and job design, and management systems and procedures) are positively integrated in the eyes of individual members of the organization.

Diversity climate is built upon these same principles and effects. The following Causal Model of a Diversity Management Climate, Performance and Results illustrates the integration of key aspects of the organization and their potential impact on a diverse workforce.

How to Calculate Diversity ROI

Causal Model of a Diversity Management Climate,

Performance and Results

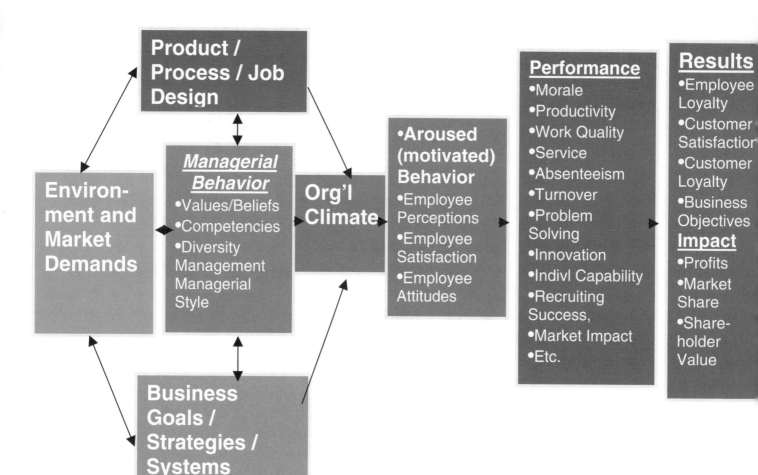

Environment and market demands create constant pressure on organizations to respond. As a result, organizations create business plan goals and strategies to meet this demand and physically structure the organization's product, process, and job design to support the goals and strategy. The person who gets to communicate all of these requirements is the manager. He or she comes to the organization with his or her own values and beliefs, technical competencies and diversity management managerial style to get the job done.

Building a Financial Performance Mindset

Depending upon the manager's use of his or her values and belief systems about people, diversity and managerial processes, he or she will create a motivating or de-motivating climate, which typically gets communicated through his or her managerial style.

The climate created by this manager will have an "instant impact" on the diverse workforce, which they experience as an aroused behavior reaction. This aroused behavior will affect their perceptions about and satisfaction level with the organizational climate and will ultimately foster a certain attitude that develops as part of the individual's behavior. This attitude will directly affect the individual's willingness to perform and therefore affects the organization's key result areas such as morale, productivity, work quality, service, absenteeism, etc. This result or lack of results will affect longer-term business results such as employee loyalty, customer loyalty, customer satisfaction, etc., which in turn will impact strategic performance areas such as profits, market share, and shareholder value.

Now that you understand how to gain management's attention using the Diversity Management Contribution Model[tm] and realize the importance of creating a solid climate for diversity management, performance, and results, lets examine some key implementation issues which are critical for success.

How to Calculate Diversity ROI

Implementation Issues

Preparing the Diversity Staff and Others To Meet the Challenge

One group that may resist the DROI process is the diversity staff who must design, develop, and implement the initiative. These staff members sometimes see evaluation as an unnecessary intrusion into their responsibilities, absorbing precious time, and stifling their freedom to be creative. One reason the diversity staff may resist the DROI process is that the effectiveness of their program will be fully exposed, putting their reputation on the line. They may have fear of failure. To overcome this, the DROI process should be positioned as a tool for learning and not a tool to evaluate the diversity staff's performance, at least during its early years of implementation. The diversity staff will not be interested in developing a process that will be used against them.

Evaluators can learn as much from failures as successes. If the diversity initiative is not working, it is best to find out quickly and understand the issues first hand---not from others. If the initiative is ineffective and not producing the results, it will eventually become known to the rest of the organization, if they are not already aware of it. A lack of results will cause management and others to become less supportive. If the weaknesses of the initiative are identified and adjustments are made quickly, not only will effective initiatives be developed, but the credibility and respect for the diversity function will be enhanced.

Removing Obstacles

Removing implementation obstacles to the DROI process is critical for success. Some of these are realistic barriers, while others are often based upon misconceptions. Each barrier should be explored and addressed. The most common are:

DROI is a complex process. Many of the diversity staff will perceive DROI studies as too complex a process to implement. To counter this, the diversity staff must understand that by breaking the process down into individual components and steps, it can be simplified.

Diversity staff members often feel they do not have time for evaluation. They need to understand that the evaluation efforts can save more time in the future. A DROI study may show that the initiative should be changed, modified, or even terminated altogether. Also, up front planning with an evaluation strategy can save additional follow-up time for the overall evaluation.

The diversity staff must be motivated to pursue evaluations, even when senior executives are not requiring it. Most diversity staff members will know when top managers are pushing the accountability issue. If they do not see that push, they are reluctant to take the time to make it work. They must see the benefits of pursuing the DROI process even if it is not required or encouraged from the top.

The diversity staff may be concerned that the DROI results will lead to criticism. Many diversity staff members will be concerned about the use of DROI study information. If the results are used to criticize or assess the performance of the initiative designers or facilitators, there will be a reluctance to embrace the concept. DROI should be considered as a learning process, at least in the early stages of implementation. Later, it should be required.

These and other obstacles can cause havoc for an otherwise successful DROI implementation. Each must be removed or reduced to a manageable issue.

Application Exercise

1. What obstacles (if any) do you anticipate?

_____

_____

_____

What to Do Next

2. How will you remove them?

_____

_____

_____

DROI is a Critical Link For Success

Calculating Diversity Return On Investment (DROI) is a critical link for success in diversity management and organizational performance in the future. "You can't manage what you don't measure" and managing and leveraging diversity is fast becoming a business imperative. If diversity initiatives are not approached in a systematic, logical, and planned way, DROI will not be possible and consequently, diversity will not become integrated into the fabric of the organization.

It is our job as diversity practitioners to make certain that the credibility of diversity efforts do not suffer. We must build a strong business practice reputation using effective diversity measurement and management techniques such that diversity is seen as a key driver of organizational performance and success!

How to Calculate Diversity ROI

Index

How to Calculate Diversity ROI

References

References

References

Bader, Gloria E, Bloom, Audrey E., Chang, Richard Y. *Measuring Team Performance.* Irvine California: Richard Chang Associates Inc. 1994.

Baytos, Lawrence M. *Designing & Implementing Successful Diversity Programs.* New Jersey: Prentice Hall. 1995.

Bramley, Peter. *Evaluating Training Effectiveness: Translating Theory into Practice.* London: McGraw-Hill. 1991.

Brown, Mark Graham, *Keeping Score,* New York: Quality Resources, 1996.

Casio, Wayne F. *Applied Psychology in Personnel Management, Second Edition.* Reston Virginia: Reston Publishing Company, Inc. 1982.

Casio, Wayne F. *Costing Human Resources: The Financial Impact of Behavior in Organizations, Second Edition.* Boston, Massachusetts: PWS-Kent Publishing Company. 1987.

Casio, Wayne F. *Managing Human Resources,* New York: McGraw-Hill. 1995.

Chang, Richard Y., Kelly, P. Keith. *Improving Through Benchmarking.* Irvine California: Richard Chang Associates Inc. 1994.

Christopher, William F., Thor, Carl G. *Handbook for Productivity Measurement and Improvement.* Portland, Oregon: Productivity Press. 1993.

References

Clardy, Alan, *Studying Your Workforce*, Newbury Park, California: Sage Publications. 1997.

Cox, Taylor Jr. *Cultural Diversity In Organizations*. San Francisco, California: Berrett-Koehler Publishers. 1993.

Craig, Robert L. *The ASTD Training & Development Handbook: A Guide To Human Resources Development*. New York: McGraw-Hill. 1996.

Edwards, Mark R., Ewen, Ann J. *360° Feedback*. New York: AMACOM. 1996.

Fink, Arlene, *The Survey Handbook*, Newbury Park, California: Sage Publications. 1995.

Fitz-enz, Jac. *How To Measure Human Resources Management, Second Edition*. New York: McGraw-Hill, Inc. 1995.
Gardenswartz, Lee, Rowe, Anita. *Diverse Teams at Work: Capitalizing on the Power of Diversity*. Chicago: Irwin Professional Publishing. 1994.

Gardenswartz, Lee, Rowe, Anita. *Managing Diversity: A Complete Desk Reference*. New York: Irwin Professional Publishing. 1993.

Gentile, Mary C. *Managerial Excellence Through Diversity*. Chicago: Irwin Professional Publishing. 1996.

Hale, Judith, *The Performance Consultant's Fieldbook*, San Francisco: Jossey-Bass/Pfeiffer, 1998

Harrington, H. James, *Area Activity Analysis*, New York: McGraw-Hill, 1999.

Harvard Business Review, *Harvard Business Review on Measuring Corporate Performance*, Boston Massachusetts: Harvard Business School Press, 1998.

References

Henerson, Marlene E., Morris, Lynn Lyons, Taylor Fitz-Gibbon, Carol. *How To Measure Attitudes*. Newbury Park, California: Sage Publications. 1987.

Heskett, James L., Sasser, Earl W., Jr., Schlesinger, Leonard A., The Service Profit Chain, New York: The Free Press, 1997.

Hubbard, Edward E. *Measuring Diversity Results*. Petaluma, California: Global Insights Publishing. 1997.

Hubbard, Edward E. *The Hidden Side Of Resistance To Change*. Petaluma, California: Global Insights Publishing. 1994.

Jackson, Susan E. and Associates. *Diversity in the Workplace*. New York: The Guilford Press. 1992.

Jamieson, David, O'Mara, Julie. *Managing Workforce 2000: Gaining the Diversity Advantage*. San Francisco, California: Jossey-Bass. 1991.

Jerome, Paul J. *Re-Creating Teams During Transitions*. Irvine California: Richard Chang Associates Inc. 1994.

Kaplan, Robert S., and Norton, David P., *The Balanced Scorecard*, Boston Massachusetts: Harvard Business School Press, 1996.

Kessler, Sheila, *Measuring and Managing Customer Satisfaction*, Milwaukee, Wisconsin: ASQC, 1996.

King, Jean A, Morris, Lynn Lyons, Taylor Fitz-Gibbon, Carol. *How To Assess Program Implementation*. Newbury Park, California: Sage Publications. 1987.

Labovitz, George, and Rosansky, Victor, *The Power of Alignment*, New York: John Wiley & Sons, 1997.

References

Litwin, George H., and Stringer, Robert A., Jr, *Motivation and Organizational Climate*, Boston, Massachusetts, Harvard University Division of Research, 1968

McCoy, Thomas J. *Compensation and Motivation*. New York: AMACOM. 1992.

Mercer, Michael W., *Turning Your Human Resources Department into a Profit Center*, New York: AMACOM, 1989.

Moran, Linda, Musselwhite, Ed, Zenger, John H. *Keeping Teams On Track*. Chicago, Illinois: Irwin Professional Publishing. 1996.

Office of Human Resources, Federal Aviation Administration. *Diversity Training Evaluation Toolkit*. Oaklahoma City, Oaklahoma: Mike Monroney Aeronautical Center. June, 1994.

Phillips, Jack J. *Handbook of Training Evaluation and Measurement Methods, Second Edition*. Houston, Texas: Gulf Publishing Company. 1991.

Phillips, Jack J. *In Action: Measuring Return On Investment, Vol. 1*, Alexandria Virginia: ASTD, 1994.

Phillips, Jack J. *In Action: Measuring Return On Investment, Vol. 2*, Alexandria Virginia: ASTD, 1997.

Rummler, Geary A., Brache, Alan P., *Improving Performance*, San Francisco, California: Jossey-Bass. 1995.

Sloma, Richard S. *How To Measure Managerial Performance*. New York: MacMillan Publishing Co., Inc. 1980.

Smith, Douglas K., *Make Success Measurable!*, New York: John Wiley & Sons, 1999.

References

Spencer, Lyle M. Jr. *Calculating Human Resource Costs and Benefits: Cutting Costs and Improving Productivity.* New York: John Wiley & Sons. 1986.

Swanson, Richard A., Holton, Elwood F., *Results,* San Francisco: Berrett-Koehler Publishers, 1999.

Taylor Fitz-Gibbon, Carol , Morris, Lynn Lyons. *How To Analyze Data.* Newbury Park, California: Sage Publications. 1987.

Thiederman, Sondra. *Bridging Cultural Barriers for Corporate Success.* Lexington, Massachusetts: Lexington, Books. 1991.

Thomas, R, Roosevelt, Jr. *Redefining Diversity.* New York: AMACOM. 1996.

Wade, Pamela A. *Measuring The Impact Of Training.* Irvine California: Richard Chang Associates Inc. 1994.

Zemke, Ron, Thomas Kramlinger. *Figuring Things Out.* Reading Massachusetts: Addison-Wesley Publishing Company, Inc. 1987.

Zigon, Jack, *How to Measure Employee Performance,* Wallingford, PA: Zigon Performance Group, 1998.

How to Calculate Diversity ROI

Additional Diversity Measurement Resources From Hubbard & Hubbard, Inc.

Additional Diversity Measurement Resources Available From Hubbard & Hubbard, Inc.

Diversity Measurement and Productivity Series Developed By Dr. Edward E. Hubbard

- "Measuring Diversity Results"
- "How To Calculate Diversity Return On Investment (DROI)"

Additional Books by Dr. Edward E. Hubbard

- "The Hidden Side of Employee Resistance to Change"
- "Managing Organizational Change"
- "Managing Customer Service On the Front-Line"
- "Internal Customer Care: Giving Effective Customer Service to Co-Workers"
- and others

Software Products

- *MetricLINK*^{tm} - Diversity measurement, tracking, and reporting tool

- ***Survey Pro^{tm}*** - Survey design, development, analysis, and reporting tool
- ***HR Stat Pak^{tm}*** – Turnover and performance appraisal impact analysis tool
- ***Seminar Analysis System^{tm}*** – Training development costs and implementation analysis tool

Hubbard & Hubbard, Inc. Diversity Measurement & Productivity Institute (DM&P) Workshops

- Measuring Diversity Results
- How To Calculate Diversity Return on Investment (DROI)
- Building a Measurable Diversity Strategic Plan
- How to Create a Diversity Culture and Systems Audit
- Assessing Diversity Training Impact
- Conducting a Cultural Due Diligence Audit
- Measuring Supplier Diversity
- How to Construct a Business Case for Diversity
- Productivity Measurement for Diverse Work Teams
- Managing Diversity Related Change Efforts
- Diversity Facts, Figures, and Financials: An Overview
- MetricLINK^{tm} Software User Training
- Survey Pro^{tm} Software User Training

Measurement Resources (Books, Video, Audio)

Books

- ***The Survey Analysis Kit*** – A 9-book resource kit for survey development and analysis
- ***The Focus Group Kit*** – A 6-book resource kit for conducting focus groups

Dr. Hubbard on Video

- Diversity: Making It Work (14mins.)
- The Roller-coaster of Change (14mins.)
- Making Teams Work (13mins.)
- Planning to Restructure (13mins)

Dr. Hubbard on Audio

- "Quantifying Diversity"
- "How to Measure Diversity Results in Hard & Soft Numbers"

Diversity Measurement Instrumentation

- ***Diversity Business Rationale Index*** – Helps identify key strategic areas to measure for diversity and the reasons that support them

- ***Managing Inclusion Analysis*** – This is a comprehensive culture and systems audit instrument

- ***Diversity Strategic Alignment Profile*** – Based on the Hubbard Diversity 9-S Framework, this profile assesses the your diversity effort's alignment in each of the key Diversity 9-S Framework areas for success

- ***Diversity Initiatives Analysis*** – This survey assesses how results-based your diversity efforts are. Great for Diversity Councils and Senior Executives

- ***Diversity Strategic Planning Readiness Check*** – This survey provides a quick assessment to determine the organization's readiness for diversity strategic planning